ISLAND COOKING

Bonnie Tuell

Mutual Publishing

Design by Cecilia Vargas
Cover design by Jane Hopkins

First Printing November 1996
Second Printing June 1997
Third Printing June 1999
Fourth Printing March 2001
Fifth Printing March 2002
Sixth Printing October 2003
6 7 8 9
ISBN 1-56647-137-0

Mutual Publishing
1215 Center Street, Suite 210
Honolulu, Hawaii 96816
Telephone (808) 732-1709
Fax (808) 734-4094
e-mail: mutual@mutualpublishing.com
www.mutualpublishing.com
Printed in Australia

Fish List

Hawaiian	Haole	Japanese	Method of Cooking
A'awa	Wrasse (Sandfish)		Fry
Ahipalaha	Bluefin Albacore	Tombishibi (Maguro)	Raw, Broil, Bake
Ahi	Yellowfin Tuna	Shibi (Maguro)	Bake, Raw, Fry, Broil, Steam
Aholehole	Seabass		Broil, Bake, Fry, Boil
Ahaaha	Needlefish	Saeri	Seldom used for food
Alaihi (Alaihi Kalaloa)			Seldom used for food
Amaama	Mullet	Ina (Bora)	Broil, Fry, Bake, Chowder
Aku	Ocean Bonito (Skipjack)	Katsuo	Fry, Dry, Raw, Boil, Chowder
Akule		Aji	Broil, Dry, Fry
A'u	Marlin (Striped Marlin)	Kajikitoshi	Bake, Fry, Chowder
A'u	Swordfish		Bake, Fry, Chowder
A'u Lepe	Sailfish	Oriental Sailfish	Bake, Fry, Chowder
Awa	Milkfish		Chowder, Fish Cake, Bake, Raw
Awa'aua	Ten Pounder		Raw, Fish Cake
Aweoweo	Big Red Eye		Fry, Broil
Hapuupuu	Black Sea Bass	Ala	Seldom used for food
He'e	Octopus	Tako	Steamed, Raw, Dry
Hihimanu	Spotted Sting Ray	Akae	
Hilu Piliko'a	Black Sided Hawkfish		
Hinalea	Green Wrasse	Gizame	Chowder, Clear Soup, Boil
Hono	Turtle	Kame	Pound and Fry
Humuhumunukunukuapua'a	Triggerfish	Hage	Cut through skin and Fry
Humuhumu 'Ele'ele	Black Triggerfish		Seldom eaten
Kahala	Amberfish	Kanapachi	
Kaku	Barracuda	Kamasu	Fry, Bake, Chowder
Kala	Doctor Fish (Unicorn)		Dry, Boil
Kalikali	Small Snapper		
Kawakawa	Bonito (Little Tunny)	Katsuo	Raw, Fry, Broil
Kikakapu	Yellow Manini		Poor eating quality
Koai		Onaga	Fry, Dry and Broil
Kole (Kale)			Fry, Dry and Broil
Kumu	Goatfish (Rose and Black)		Broil, Steam, Fry, Bake, Boil
Kupipi	Spot Pom		Fry
Lehi	Snapper		Fry, Broil, Bake, Steam
Lai			Not usually eaten, dry meat
Lae-Nihi	Longfin Razorfish	Nabeta	Broil, Fry
Mahimahi	Dolphin	Mansaku	Fry, Chowder, Broil, Bake
Maiko (Maiko Iko)			Dry and Broil
Malolo	Flying Fish	Tombo Uo	Fry, Broil
Malu	Goatfish (Rose and Yellow with black spots)		Fry, Bake, Broil
Mamo (Mao Mao)	Banded Damselfish		Fry, Broil
Manini	Tang		Fry, Broil, Dry
Mano (Niuhi)	Shark	Fuka	Fish Cake, Dry and Broil
Mano Kihikihi	Hammerhead Shark	Kasebuka	Fish Cake, Dry and Broil
Moano	Goatfish		Fry, Bake
Moi	Threadfish		Bake, Fry, Steam, Raw
Mu		Medai	Raw, Fry, Boil, Broil
Muhee	Squid	Ika	Steam, Boil
Nehu	Shiner	Iriko	Used as bait
Nenui (Manaloa)			Boil, Fry
Nohu		Okode	Fry, Clear soup, Chowder
'O'io	Bonefish (Ladyfish)		Raw, Fish Cake, Clear soup
Omaka (Amuku, Makiawa)			Fry, Dry
Omilu	Blue Crevally		Bread and Fry, Raw
Ono	Wahoo	Sawara	Fry, Bake, Broil, Steam, Soup
Opae	Shrimp	Ebi (Koebi)	Pan roast until red

Hawaiian	Haole	Japanese	Method of Cooking
Oʻopuhue (Maki-maki)	Balloon Fish	Fugu	Not to be eaten; poisonous
Opakapaka	Pink Snapper		Broil, Bake, Coddle, Fry
Opelu	Small Mackerel Family	Saba	Bake in shoyu, Raw, Dry
Opihi	Limpet	Awabi	Raw
Pakii	Flounder	Kare	Dry and Broil
Paoʻo (Panoʻa)		Gori	Not used as food
Papai	Crab	Kani	Boil
Papio	Pampano		Fry, Raw
Pauuʻu (Hon-ulua)			Bread and Fry
Pilikoʻa	White Lined Hawkfish		Chowder
Poʻopaʻa	Rock Cod		Chowder, Fry, Broil
Pualu	Surgeonfish	Hage	Dry and Broil
Puhi	Brown Eel	Unagi	Delicacy when broiled
Puhi Uha	White Eel		Delicacy when broiled
Uhu	Parrot Fish		Bake, Clear soup
Uku	Snapper		Bake, Broil, Chowder, Steam
Ula	Lobster	Iscebi	Broil, Steam
Ulae		Sunakakure	Fish Cake, Chowder
Ulaula	Snapper		Fry, Broil, Bake, Steam
Ukihikihi	Moorish Idol		Fry, Broil
Ulua (Lauli, Black Ulua)	Jack Crevally		Raw, Steam, Fry, Broil, Bake
Ulua Pauu (Paopao, Striped Ulua)			Fry
Ulua (White Ulua)	White Ulua		Bread and Fry, Broil, Raw
Ulua Kihikihi	Silver Ulua	Kagami-Ulua	Fry
Upapalu			Fry, Broil
Uouoa	Net Fish		Dry and Broil
Uʻu	Red Squirrelfish	Mempachi	Fry, Steam, Broil, Boil
Weke	Goatfish (Pink and White)		Fry, Broil, Bake, Boil
	Cod	Tara	Fry, Bake

. . . .

Table of Weight & Measures

3 teaspoons = 1 tablespoon
16 tablespoons = 1 cup
5/8 cup = 1/2 cup + 2 tablespoons
7/8 cup = 1 cup – 2 tablespoons
2 cups = 1 pint
2 pints = 1 quart
1/2 cup margarine = 1 block
2 cups shortening = 1 pound
2 cups granulated sugar = 1 pound
4 cups flour = 1 pound
1 square chocolate = 1 ounce
1/4 cup cocoa = 1 ounce
16 ounces = 1 pound

Substitutions

1 c sour milk = 1 c – 1 T milk + 1 T vinegar or lemon juice
1 c buttermilk = 1 c – 1 T milk + 1 T vinegar or lemon juice
1 c butter = 1 c margarine (oleo) or 7/8 c shortening + 1/4 t salt
1 square (1 oz.) chocolate = 1/4 c unsweetened bakers cocoa + 1 T shortening
1 c heavy cream = 5/6 c milk + 1/3 c shortening
1 c cake flour = 1 c – 2 T regular flour

Key

❖—Freeze	T—tablespoon	t—teaspoon
c—cup	lb.—pound	pkg.—package
oz.—ounce	gal.—gallon	qt.—quart

Ingredients

All are level measurements. Dry foods in nested metal cups; liquid foods in glass spouted cups.

Brown sugar **always** means boxed light or dark brown sugar. Raw sugar means washed or coarse sugar.

MSG means monosodium glutamate such as Accent, Ajinomoto, or Vitsin. Hawaiian salt means rock salt. Regular flour need not e sifted if it is lightly spooned in the cup, then leveled. Do not scoop or flour will pack.

Powdered sugar is also called confectioners sugar.

Some Don'ts on Freezing

All but a few precooked foods can be frozen successfully. It is therefore well to discuss the "don'ts," since this is a much shorter list. These are the foods which cannot be handled successfully, and the reasons why:

Cooked potatoes (except stuffed baked potatoes, mashed potato patties) lose texture when frozen. It is best to add them to a prepared main dish when the food is reheated for serving.

Rice, noodles and macaroni tend to lose texture, become extra soft. These foods cooked, then frozen in sauce sufficient to cover them seem to retain a desirable texture.

Creamed foods, puddings, fillings and cream sauces thickened with regular flour or corn starch tend to separate and become watery.

Cream and custard pies are not suitable for freezing. Baked or boiled custards made by home-type recipes separate with a curdled effect.

Gelatin desserts and salads "weep" when thawed.

Cooked meats with considerable fat tend to develop rancidity of the fat. (Extensive trimming off of fat before freezing helps to prevent this.)

Hard-cooked egg whites become leathery, rubbery and tough. The exception to this is when the egg white, chopped, is added to sandwich filling. Raw egg white freezes very well.

Salad greens lose their crispness, and crisp celery, carrots, raw apples (all in chunky pieces) grapes, tomatoes and bananas develop a gummy texture when frozen. Very finely chopped celery may be frozen as sandwich filling ingredients.

Mayonnaise and similar emulsified foods separate when frozen.

High Altitude Rules for Baking

Up to 3,000 feet, if you reduce the air in the cake by not overbeating eggs, you will probably need no adjustment of the recipe. Raise the baking temperature about 25°. In elevations higher than 3,000 feet, continue to underbeat the eggs as compared to sea level consistency. Another way to reduce their volume is to keep eggs refrigerated until almost ready to use. At around 5,000 feet, it will help to reduce the double-acting baking powder by 1/8 to 1/4 teaspoon for each teaspoon called for in the recipe. Decrease sugar 1 to 2 tablespoons for each cup called for. Increase liquid 2 to 3 tablespoons for each cup indicated. Raise the baking temperature 25°.

Angel and sponge cakes: Reduce sugar about 1 tablespoon for each 1,000 feet above 3,000 feet.

Popovers: Add one extra egg, decrease shortening by 1/2 to 1 tablespoon.

Candy and frosting: Decrease boiling temperature 1.9° for each 1,000 feet above sea level. To determine the exact boiling temperature of a given altitude, check thermometer in boiling water. Subtract this reading from 212°. This will be the adjustment you will make on the final reading for any recipe. The commonly used cold-water tests can naturally be used for syrups to be cooked to the right consistency of soft ball, hard ball, crack, etc. stages. It is wise to cook candies and frosting to a slightly firmer stage on rainy, humid days.

Freezing: Scald or steam the vegetables for the specified number of minutes plus one-half minute more for each 1,000 feet over 2,000 feet above sea level.

Puddings and cream pie fillings: Direct heat, rather than the double boiler method, will help to provide maximum gelatinization of the starch and give more satisfactory products.

Yeast breads: Less flour (1 tablespoon per cup) is needed to compensate for greater evaporation at higher altitude.

Cookies: Soft cookies require 1/2 teaspoon less baking powder. Rich, crisp cookies need 1 tablespoon per cup less sugar.

Quick breads: Decrease baking powder 1/8 to 1/4 teaspoon.

Table of Contents

Artichoke

❖ You may cook artichokes as directed, remove all leaves and freeze artichoke hearts that have been dipped in lemon juice.

How to Prepare and Cook Artichokes:

To Clean: Hold artichoke by stem and dash up and down quickly in deep bowl of water. Pull off tough row of bottom leaves and cut stem even with base of artichoke. Cut one inch from top leaves to eliminate stickers. You may dip cut parts in lemon juice to prevent discoloration.

To Cook: Place artichoke, stem end down, in one inch of water in large pot. Cover and cook 25 to 30 minutes or until heart is tender. You may add any or a combination of the following:

I slice onion or I clove mashed garlic
Celery leaves
1-1/2 T lemon juice, wine or vinegar
2 T salad oil
I bay leaf

When tender, remove from water. Serve hot with lemon butter, plain melted butter, mayonnaise or Hollandaise sauce.

To Eat: Serve one to each person. The leaves are pulled off, one at a time, and dipped in sauce. The lower end is pulled through the teeth to extract the tender, edible portion. The leaf is then discarded. Continue to eat them until a light-colored cone of young leaves appears. Pull entire cone up with one movement and discard. Then lift the fuzzy center out and discard it. Eat the remaining heart with a fork, dipping each piece in sauce first.

CHICKEN-ARTICHOKE CASSEROLE

Yield: 6 servings

3 lb. cut-up fryer (or equal weight of chicken pieces)
1-1/2 t salt
1/2 t paprika
1/2 t pepper
6 T butter
1/4 lb. mushrooms, cut in large pieces
12–15 oz. can artichoke hearts
2 T flour
2/3 c chicken consommé or bouillon
3 T sherry

Salt, pepper and paprika the chicken pieces. Then brown them in 4 tablespoons of butter and put them in a big casserole. Put the other 2 tablespoons of butter into the frying pan and sauté the mushrooms in it for five minutes.

Then sprinkle the flour over mushrooms and stir in chicken consommé and sherry. While this cooks five minutes, open the can of artichokes and arrange between the chicken pieces. Pour the mushroom-sherry sauce over the chicken, cover and bake at 375° for 40 minutes.

STUFFED ARTICHOKE

Cook as directed above. Remove center portion of leaves and fuzzy center of heart. Fill with creamed meat or fish or a filling used for eggplant in this book. Bake for 15 minutes at 350° or until filling is very hot.

Avocado

❖ Freeze only sieved, raw purée. For molded salads, ice cream or sherbet, add 1-1/2 tablespoons sugar and 2 teaspoons lemon juice to each cup. For sandwiches, salad dressings, or dips, omit sugar and add onion juice, salt and pepper to taste, along with 2 teaspoons lemon juice to each cup.

Hint: Avocados are ready to pick when the stems swell a little.
Calories: One-half Summer—144; One-half Winter—490

BAKED AVOCADOS

Have as many avocados as persons to be served if the avocados are small. If very large, allow one-half per person. Remove seeds and if the opening is too small, scoop out a little of the pear. Fill the cavities with favorite creamed fish, well seasoned (crab, lobster or tuna). Sprinkle grated cheese lightly on top and bake about 15 minutes at 350°F.

AVOCADO SANDWICH SPREAD

Take two large avocados, peel and remove seeds and inner skin. Put through a food ricer or sieve. Add 1 tablespoon lemon juice, 1 level teaspoon garlic salt, 1 tablespoon A-1 sauce and a dash of red pepper. Stir thoroughly and chill.

TUNA-AVOCADO SANDWICH FILLING

Mash one avocado, combine with one can tuna. Season with salt and sugar.

AVOCADO DIP

Yield: 1/3 cup

I c avocado pulp
I t salt
dash of pepper
1-1/2 t lemon juice
1-1/2 t onion, grated
sliced cucumber
paprika

Combine avocado, salt, pepper, lemon juice and onion. Blend thoroughly. Serve on potato chips, crackers or on sliced cucumbers topped with a dash of paprika.

Chiyoko Wong's Avocado Apple Mold

Yield: 8 servings

1 3 oz. lemon flavored gelatin
1 c very hot water
1 c mayonnaise
2 Golden Delicious apples, peeled and diced
    to equal 1 cup
1-1/2 T lemon juice
1 t salt
3/4 c avocado, peeled and sieved
1/4 c almonds, slivered (optional)
1/4 c heavy cream, whipped
slices of apple and avocado for garnish

Dissolve gelatin in boiling water. Chill until syrupy, then whip until fluffy. Fold in mayonnaise, diced apple, sprinkled with lemon juice, salt. Fold in sieved avocado and whipped cream. Pour into 4-quart mold rinsed with cold water. Chill until firm. Unmold on flat, round platter and garnish with apple and avocado slices, both dipped in lemon juice.

Avocado Chiffon Pie

1 9" pie shell, baked
1 c strained avocado
3 eggs, separated
1-1/2 T butter
1/2 t nutmeg
1 t cinnamon
1/2 c sugar
Juice of 1/2 lemon (1-1/2 T)
1 envelope plain gelatin
1/4 c cold water
1/2 c sugar
whipped cream (sweetened)

Combine avocado pulp, egg yolks, butter, nutmeg, cinnamon, 1/2 cup sugar and lemon juice in saucepan and bring to a boil. Soften gelatin in 1/4 cup cold water. Add to hot mixture. Cool mixture and fold in three egg whites beaten with 1/2 cup sugar. Pour into baked pie shell and chill thoroughly. Top with sweetened whipped cream.

Bamboo Shoots and Fern Shoots

In a bamboo forest, look for shoots sprouting from the ground. Break off with the foot. Peel off fuzzy skin. Boil until tender. Cut in half lengthwise. Soak two to three days, changing water occasionally to remove bitter taste.

❖ Freeze either cooked in plain water or in meat dish already cooked and seasoned. Use in chop suey, sukiyaki or other shoyu dishes.

Calories: 1 cup—37

Chinese Spring Rolls (good pupu)

2 c bamboo shoots, cut in strips lengthwise
3 c bean sprouts
3 T oil
2 T onion, chopped
1/2 c dried mushrooms, prepared*
1 lb. ground pork
3 T shoyu
1 T sherry
1 T cornstarch
1 t salt
1 T fresh ginger, chopped
2 pkg. wun tun pi
1/2 c cold water
1 T cornstarch
oil for deep frying

*To prepare mushrooms: rinse well, cover with lukewarm water, let stand 15 to 20 minutes until spongy. Squeeze, but save water. Cut in strips after removing stems.

Sauté bamboo shoots in 1 tablespoon oil. Add bean sprouts and heat thoroughly. Add 2 tablespoons shoyu and continue to sauté for a few minutes, then remove from pan. Reheat pan, add 1 tablespoon oil and sauté onion and mushrooms; remove from pan. Combine pork with 1 tablespoon shoyu, sherry, cornstarch and salt. Reheat pan, add 1 tablespoon oil and sauté pork mixture until thoroughly cooked. Add vegetables and ginger. Cool.

Moisten three sides of wun tun pi with mixture of 1 tablespoon cornstarch and water. Place 2 teaspoons meat-vegetable mixture on unmoistened end. Turn up bottom edge over filling, fold side edges in and roll in log form. Deep fry until brown. Freeze excess uncooked, if desired.

Kalua Pig with Chinese Vegetables

2 lb. kalua pig
1 c onions, sliced
2 c bamboo shoots, sliced
7 dried mushrooms, soaked and sliced
8 water chestnuts, sliced
4 T shoyu
1 T sugar
1 T cornstarch
1/2 c mushroom water
1 t black pepper
dash salt
dash Ajinomoto
1 T sherry or bourbon

Fry kalua pig in fry pan until hot, add sliced onions and fry until almost tender. Push to side of pan. In oil remaining, fry bamboo shoots, then mix into first mixture. Push to side of pan and sauté mushrooms until coated with oil, then combine with first mixture. Sauté water chestnuts in same manner and combine. Mix shoyu, sugar, cornstarch, mushroom water, pepper, salt, Aji and sherry. Stir into vegetables and cook until thickened. Serve hot.

CHICKEN AND BAMBOO SHOOTS

Yield: 6 servings

2 lb. chicken thighs
2 T butter
3/4 c shoyu
1/2 c raw sugar
3 T mirin
1/2 t MSG
2 c bamboo shoots (either canned or fresh),
    sliced, or fern shoots
1 6-1/3 oz. can button mushrooms
2 c watercress in 1" pieces

Chicken may be deboned and cut into one-inch square cubes, chopped in half crosswise, or left whole. Sauté in butter about five minutes. Combine shoyu, sugar, mirin and MSG. Pour over chicken. Cook 15 to 20 minutes, or until chicken is done. Stir in bamboo shoots and button mushrooms. Cook another five minutes. Stir with watercress, remove immediately from heat. Serve hot with rice.

Banana

❖ Bananas have a marked tendency to darken and to lose texture; tend to develop off-flavors. Cooked bananas make excellent frozen products if cooked before freezing. Raw purée may be frozen, with lemon juice added to prevent discoloration. Chocolate-dipped bananas are good if eaten while still frozen.

Cooking bananas are rounder, smoother and have rounded ends.
Calories: 4-1/2 "—110
Eating bananas are long, slim and have length-wise ridges.
Calories: 7"—123

FROZEN BANANA STICKS

Yield: 8 servings

2 c corn flakes or
1/2 c packaged corn flake crumbs
8 wooden skewers
1 c (6 oz.) semi-sweet chocolate pieces
4 ripe bananas

Crush corn flakes into fine crumbs. Melt chocolate over hot but not boiling water. Peel bananas and cut in half crosswise. Place skewer in end of each half. Spread with melted chocolate; roll in corn flake crumbs. Place on waxed paper-lined baking sheet and freeze.

Baked Bananas

Select fully ripe cooking bananas or eating bananas which are ripe but firm. Place in a shallow pan and bake at 350°F. For eating bananas, allow 20 to 30 minutes and for cooking bananas, allow 45 minutes. Split skin and serve plain or with lemon or lime juice and butter.

Fried Bananas

Peel and cut bananas in halves crosswise, then lengthwise. Sprinkle with lemon juice. Fry quickly in butter until a delicate brown. Serve at once.

Glazed Bananas

Peel ripe bananas and dip in lemon juice. Roll in sugar and sauté slowly in butter until tender, turning to brown evenly. Serve hot as a vegetable.

Green Banana Salad

Yield: 8 to 10 servings

8–10 Chinese or Bluefield green bananas
1/4 c carrots, grated
1/4 c celery, grated
2 T onion, grated
1/2 bell pepper, minced
1 T salad oil
1 T vinegar
1/4 t MSG
salt and pepper
mayonnaise

Boil bananas in jackets in salted water to cover until skins burst. Drain, cool. Peel and dice bananas. Combine bananas, carrots, celery, onions, peppers in a bowl. Add salad oil, vinegar, MSG, salt and pepper to taste. Add enough mayonnaise to moisten. Chill before serving.

Banana Bread in Electric Skillet

1/2 c nuts, chopped
1 c banana, mashed
1-2/3 c sifted flour
1 t soda
1/2 t salt
1/2 c soft butter
1 c sugar
2 eggs
1 t vanilla
1/4 c buttermilk

Preheat covered fry pan to 420° with vent closed. If using oven, bake at 350°F for one hour. Grease and flour four empty No. 2 size cans or a 9x9-inch square pan.

Chop nuts. Mash bananas. Sift flour, soda and salt together. Combine butter, sugar, eggs and vanilla in large mixer bowl. Cream on high speed of mixer for 1 to 1-1/2 minutes. Stop, scrape bowl, add nuts, banana, buttermilk and flour mixture. Beat on low speed about half a minute until well blended. Fill cans two-thirds full. Set on rack. Bake about one hour, opening vent last 10 minutes. Loosen and remove from pans. Cool thoroughly before slicing.

Surprise Banana Cake

1 Duncan Hines Spice Cake Mix
3/4 c water minus 2 tablespoons
2 T oil
1/2 t baking powder
2 eggs
1 c banana, mashed

Blend all ingredients on low mixer speed, then beat two minutes on high speed. Pour into two oiled, waxed paper-lined 8-inch cake pans or one 9x15x2-inch pan. Bake at 350°F 25 to 30 minutes. Frost with Mock Whipped Cream Icing.

Jello Kanten

2 3 oz. boxes flavored gelatin
4 pkg. unflavored gelatin
1/2 c cold water
1 c sugar
5 c hot water

Add cold water to gelatin to soften. Add jello, sugar and hot water. Stir until dissolved. Refrigerate until jello is set. Fruits and fruit juices may be added. Try sliced bananas, mangoes, or guava shells. Do not use fresh or frozen pineapple because an enzyme eats gelatin preventing setting.

Mock Whipped Cream Icing

5 T flour
1 c milk
1 t vanilla
1 c granulated sugar
1/2 c butter or margarine

Boil flour and milk until thick paste is formed. Cool thoroughly. Cream butter, sugar and vanilla. Whip together to spreading consistency.

Beans and Bean Sprouts

❖ Immerse 1 pound freshly picked green or wax beans in 1 gallon boiling water for one minute; immerse in ice water one minute; package and freeze.

Immerse 1 pound slightly underripe lima beans in 1 gallon boiling water for 1-1/2 minutes; immerse in ice water 1-1/2 minutes; package and freeze.

Do not freeze bean sprouts.

Green beans: Spices and herbs can enhance, even "change" any vegetable. Try these subtle tools for enlivening string beans: basil, garlic salt, dried dill, marjoram or savory. Or add pimientos, garlic croutons, green pepper, browned mushrooms—fresh or canned—or any kind of slivered nuts.

STRING BEANS MISO AE

Yield: 4 servings

1 lb. string beans
2 T sesame seeds, toasted
2 T miso (fermented bean curd)
2 T sugar
1/3 c mayonnaise
1/4 t MSG

Cut string beans into one-inch pieces. Boil until tender in 1/2 cup water (about 15 or 20 minutes); drain. Mash sesame seeds in suribachi (grinding bowl) or use blender. Add miso, sugar, MSG and mayonnaise. Blend well and mix with string beans. Serve either warm or chilled.

COMPANY GREEN BEAN CASSEROLE

Yield: 8 servings

2 12 oz. pkg. frozen French-cut green beans
or 2 lb. fresh French-cut green beans
1 can cream of mushroom soup, undiluted
1 can French fried onion rings

Cook green beans until tender, drain slightly and place in casserole dish. Spoon soup onto beans and spread evenly. Top with French fried onions. Bake at 350° for 20 minutes or until dinner is ready. These will be fine up to one hour in the oven.

SWEET SOUR GREEN BEANS

Yield: 6 servings

1 lb. fresh green beans, cooked
1-1/2 c bean liquid and water
4 slices bacon
3 T sugar
2 T cornstarch
3 T vinegar
1 T shoyu
1/4 c sweet pickles, chopped
1 green pepper, sliced

Drain beans; save liquid and add enough water to make it 1-1/2 cups liquid. Fry bacon until crisp; drain and break into small pieces. Add to beans. Mix together sugar, cornstarch, vinegar and shoyu, stir into bean liquid. Add pickles and green pepper. Bring to a boil, stirring until sauce thickens and pepper is partially tender. Add beans and bacon. Simmer for one minute; serve hot.

Filipino String Beans

Yield: 6 servings

1/3 lb. pork, chopped
2 cloves garlic, crushed
1 T bagoon or shoyu
1-1/4 c water
2 lb. Filipino green beans, cut in 2" pieces
1/2 t MSG
1 small tomato, chopped

Fry pork until oil is formed. If pork is lean, add margarine or oil. Brown garlic. Add bagoon (or shoyu) and water. Bring to a boil, add beans and cook 8 to 10 minutes. Add tomato, sprinkle with MSG. Stir to combine flavors.

Pork Chops and Beans

Yield: 4 to 8 servings, depending on number of chops

4–8 large pork chops
salt and pepper
1/4 c onion, minced
1 clove garlic, minced
1 T brown sugar
1/2 t dry mustard
1 1 lb. 4 oz. can kidney beans
1 1 lb. 4 oz. can lima beans
1/4 c catsup
2 T vinegar

Brown chops, season with salt and pepper, and remove from pan. To fat in pan, add onion and garlic; sauté until tender. Add remaining ingredients and mix well. Taste and season of necessary. Pour into a 2-quart casserole, arrange chops on top and bake at 325°F for 45 minutes.

Delicious Bean Salad

Yield: 10 to 12 servings

1 1 lb. 4 oz. can garbanzo beans
1 1 lb. 4 oz. can red kidney beans
1 1 lb. 4 oz. can green beans
1 1 lb. 4 oz. can wax beans
1 onion, chopped
1 green pepper, chopped
2/3 c salad oil
1 c vinegar
1-1/2 c sugar
2 t-salt
1 t-pepper

Drain and rinse all beans. Heat remaining ingredients until sugar dissolves. Cool, then pour over beans. Marinate 24 hours in refrigerator before serving.

Green Beans Italian Style

Yield: 6 to 8 servings

2 9 oz. pkg. frozen French-cut or
    cut Italian green beans
boiling salted water
2 medium-size onions, finely chopped
1/4 c salad oil
2 T parsley, chopped
1/4 t garlic purée
1/4 c creamed cottage cheese
1/2 c Cheddar cheese, shredded
4 eggs, beaten
1/2 t salt
pepper to taste
1 c soft bread crumbs

Cook green beans in boiling, salted water until tender. In large skillet, brown onions in oil. Remove from heat and mix in parsley, garlic, cottage cheese, Cheddar cheese, eggs, salt, pepper and bread crumbs. Mix well. Layer one-half the beans in the bottom of a 12x7-inch greased baking dish. Spoon over one-half the stuffing mixture, make a second layer of the remaining beans and top with the remaining stuffing. Bake in a moderate oven (350°) for 20 minutes, or until the top is golden brown.

Chow Fun

6 c boiled noodles (look fun) cut in 1/2" to 3/4" slices
1/2 lb. chopped pork (not ground)
2 c bean sprouts
1 stalk celery (optional)
1 c string beans (optional)
2 stalks green onion, cut in 1/2" lengths

Seasonings:
1 1" piece ginger root
2 t salt
1/2 t sugar
2 T shoyu
1/4 t MSG

Garnish:
2 eggs and/or 1/4 lb. ham
2 T sesame seeds, roasted
Chinese parsley

Cut green beans and celery in thin strips if you are using them. Heat pan, add oil and heat until almost smoking. Fry pork for one minute. Add seasonings and sauté one minute. Add noodles and stir two minutes. Add string beans, celery, bean sprouts and green onion and cook until vegetables are done. Do not overcook vegetables.

Beat eggs; fry very thin. Cut ham and eggs into thin shreds. Put noodles on platter and garnish with ham and eggs, sesame seeds and Chinese parsley. Serve hot.

Berries

❖ Blackberries, mulberries and strawberries:

1.Freeze whole with just a sprinkling of sugar. Use partially frozen, if possible.

2.Freeze pulp with 1 tablespoon sugar for each cup pulp. Use for pies, jams, jellies, ice cream or cake toppings, and juices.

Jams or Jellies: Buy powdered or liquid pectin. Follow directions given with pectin.

FRESH BERRY PIE

Pastry for two-crust pie
2/3–3/4 c granulated sugar
2 T flour or 1-1/2 T tapioca
1/2 t lemon rind, grated
1–2 t lemon juice
1/4 t nutmeg
1/2 t cinnamon
1/8 t salt
4 c berries
1 T butter or margarine

Line 9-inch pie plate with pastry. Heat oven to 425°F. Combine all ingredients except berries and butter. Place half of berries in lined pie plate, sprinkle with half of sugar mixture. Repeat. Dot with butter. Cover with top crust that has 1/2-inch slashes in six places. Glaze with undiluted evaporated milk or ice water and sprinkle lightly with granulated sugar. Bake 40 to 50 minutes or until center liquid bubbles and crust is nicely browned.

UNCOOKED BERRY JAM

Wash, stem and crush enough berries to make 4 level cups. Put berries into large kettle. Slowly add one (3-1/2 ounce) package powdered pectin, stirring vigorously. Set aside for 30 minutes.

Add 1 cup light corn syrup. Mix well. Measure 5-1/2 cups sugar into dry dish. Stir this gradually into crushed berries. Warming to 100°F (no hotter) will help sugar dissolve. Bottle in sterile jars and refrigerate or freeze.

THIMBLEBERRIES

These small, pink, strawberry-like berries are found in abundance in rainy areas. They are similar to the Lingonberries in Sweden. Best eaten as found, thimbleberries are conveniently rainwashed. They add a special sparkle to salads or can be made into jelly with the addition of pectin. Use recipe for other berry jellies.

Breadfruit

Breadfruit flavor changes as it ripens. Green and hard breadfruit is very starchy and is either baked or boiled until tender. Half-ripe breadfruit is soft to the touch, but still green. Ripe breadfruit is soft, yellow-green in color and strangely sweet in flavor.

Before peeling green breadfruit, rub hands with cooking oil. This prevents stains from the white juice. Do not get this white liquid on good clothing. It will not come off.

Calories: 3/4 cup green—119; 3/4 cup ripe—268

❖ Cooked green breadfruit freezes well, but must be reheated or steamed before use. Sieved ripe breadfruit needs 1 tablespoon lemon juice per cut to prevent darkening while frozen.

Breadfruit Cake

1/2 c butter
1-1/2 c sugar
1 egg
1/2 c sour milk
2 c flour
1 t baking powder
1/4 t salt
1-1/4 t soda
3/4–1 c ripe breadfruit, mashed
2 t vanilla

Cream sugar and butter until light. Add egg and mashed breadfruit. Add sifted dry ingredients alternately with sour milk. Start and end with flour. Bake in a loaf pan at 350° for one hour.

Breadfruit and Coconut Pudding (Papaiee)

3 c ripe breadfruit
1-1/2 t salt
1 c sugar
1-1/2 c coconut milk OR 1-1/3 c lemon juice
    and 2 t ginger juice
cinnamon (optional)

Scrape pulp from soft ripe breadfruit, add lemon and ginger or coconut milk, salt and sugar. Pour into buttered baking dish. Sprinkle with cinnamon. Bake one hour in 350° oven.

Boiled Breadfruit

4 c green breadfruit, diced
3 c water
1 t salt
pepper
3 or 4 t butter

Boil water, add salt and breadfruit and boil until tender—about one hour. Drain and add seasoning and butter. This may be served in place of potatoes.

BREADFRUIT CHIPS

Peel and quarter green breadfruit. Remove core, but leave as much lacy middle as possible. Slice thin with vegetable peeler. Fry in deep oil until slightly browned and crisp. Drain on absorbent paper and salt while still hot. Store in airtight containers.

BREADFRUIT CHIFFON PIE

1 10" pie shell, baked
1 T (1 envelope) unflavored gelatin
1/4 c cold water
3 egg yolks
1/4 c sugar
1/4 t salt
1-1/2 c milk
1 t vanilla
10–12 drops yellow food color
3 egg whites
1/4 c sugar
1/4 t cream of tartar
1-1/2 c ripe breadfruit, strained
sweetened whipped cream for garnish

Sprinkle gelatin over water to soften. In double boiler or heavy pan combine yolks, 1/4 cup sugar and salt; gradually stir in milk. Cook over low heat stirring constantly just until mixture thickens slightly and coats metal spoon; remove from heat. Add softened gelatin, vanilla and food color. Cool. Add breadfruit. Add cream of tartar to egg whites. Beat until foamy, then gradually add 1/4 cup sugar while beating until whites stand in soft peaks. Fold into cooled pudding mixture. Pour into cooled pie shell. Garnish with whipped cream.

Broccoli

❖ Immerse 1 pound cleaned broccoli in salt water for 15 minutes to remove insects. Scald in 1 gallon boiling water for three minutes. Dip in ice water for two minutes, package and freeze.

Hints: Pull off tough skin from stem to cut down cooking time. Serve with butter or cheese sauce as vegetable.

BROCCOLI—CHINESE STYLE

Wash broccoli, peel stem and slice in 1/4- to 1/2-inch slices diagonally. Include leaves and heads. Heat pan very hot, add 2 tablespoons oil. When oil begins to smoke, add 1 teaspoon rock salt and 1 clove crushed garlic. Quickly add broccoli. Stir-fry until just wilted. Serve immediately.

BEEF BROCCOLI

  1 lb. meat, sliced
  2 T shoyu
  2 t sugar
  1 T ginger, crushed
  2 T sherry or whiskey
  2 T flour
  2 T oil
  2 lb. broccoli, sliced
  1/2 t salt
  1/2 c water

Marinate meat with shoyu, sugar, ginger, sherry and flour. Heat 1 tablespoon oil and stir-fry broccoli; add salt. When broccoli is slightly wilted, remove. Stir-fry meat in 1 tablespoon heated oil for two minutes. Add broccoli and water, simmer until liquid is slightly thickened.

CHOW MEIN

Yield: 6 to 8 servings

  1/2 pkg. Poppy brand noodles, cooked
  1 lb. meat (chicken, pork, beef or combination)
  12 dried mushrooms, soaked
  1 small or 1/2 large cauliflower
  1 carrot
  4 stalks celery
  10 green beans (optional)
  1/2 can bamboo shoots
  10 water chestnuts
  1 c broccoli, sliced thin OR 1 c green Chinese peas, unshelled
  1/2 c green onions
  1 clove garlic, crushed
  salt
  oil

  Sauce:
  2 t shoyu
  1 t sherry
  1 piece ginger, crushed
  pinch of five spice (optional)

  Gravy:
  1 T sugar
  1 T cornstarch
  1 c meat stock or water
  2 t shoyu
  dash of MSG

Cook noodles, rinse, drain and let cool slightly. Marinate meat in sauce. Chop vegetables. Heat 1 tablespoon oil in fry pan. Stir-fry cooked noodles until glossy. Remove to large platter. Add another tablespoon oil, heat until quite hot and sauté the clove of garlic until browned; remove garlic. Add meat and brown thoroughly. Add vegetables in order as listed. Salt to taste. When vegetables are still crisp, place over noodles. Make gravy in same pan and pour over vegetables and noodles. Garnish with egg strips or Chinese parsley.

Cabbage

❖ Cabbage cannot be frozen, but can be preserved in other ways.

Hint: Head cabbage is excellent in fruit or vegetable salads. Cooked, it may be used buttered, with miso sauce or mustard sauce, scalloped with cheese and potato chips, or used with meat in many dishes. **Chinese cabbage** (Won bok or celery cabbage) can be used in tossed salads, fried with bacon or ham for a vegetable dish, or in preserved cabbage.

CHINESE CABBAGE SOUP (WON BOK)

1 lb. pork, thinly sliced
2 t oil
8 dried shrimps
1 strip chung choi, washed
won bok
green onions, finely cut

Put oil in heated pot and cook until it smokes. Stir-fry pork until it is light brown. Add 6 cups of water, dried shrimps, chung choi and boil for 30 minutes. Add salt to taste and a dash of MSG. Add won bok which has been washed and cut into 1-1/2-inch lengths. Cook until just tender. Garnish with green onions and serve.

Canned abalone may be used to add flavor. Add liquid of abalone to stock and boil together. Slice abalone and add to soup just before serving. Do not boil abalone, as boiling toughens it.

KIMCH'I (PICKLED CABBAGE)

Yield: 1 quart

1-1/2–2 lbs. celery cabbage
1/2 crock salt
1 c water, if desired
2 t red pepper, chopped fine
1 T sugar
2–3 cloves garlic, chopped fine
1/2 t ginger root, chopped, or juice of 1" piece ginger
1/4 medium-size onion, diced

Wash cabbage and cut into 1-1/2-inch lengths. Wilt with salt for at least two hours. Water may be added to speed wilting action. Rinse cabbage and pack into glass jar. Add remaining ingredients. Cover and age two to three days before eating.

CHINESE PICKLED CABBAGE

2 large green mustard cabbage
2 c water
2 T salt
2 T vinegar
2 T sugar

Wash and drain cabbage. Separate leaves and wilt by dipping in a pot of boiling water. Drain. Cut into 1/2 to 1-inch pieces. Pack in quart jar. Combine water, salt, vinegar and sugar in saucepan. Bring to boil and pour over cabbage. Let stand two days at room temperature to develop flavor. Refrigerate until ready to use.

CABBAGE TSUKEMONO (JAPANESE PICKLED CABBAGE)

I head cabbage
1/2 t salt
I c sugar
1/2 c vinegar
I T MSG

Slice cabbage in 1/2-inch strips. Boil remaining ingredients together. Cool. Pour over cabbage. Leave overnight in refrigerator before eating. Will stay good several weeks.

Carrots

❖ Clean carrots for freezing. Slice in 1/4-inch slices. Scald in boiling water three minutes. Dip in ice water for three minutes. Package and freeze. To serve, cook covered in a small amount of boiling salted water about 10 minutes or until tender.

SPEEDY CARROT MUFFINS

Yield: 12 muffins

I heaping cup biscuit mix
I t baking soda
I t cinnamon
1/4 t salt
1/4 c nutmeats, chopped
1/4 c salad oil
1/2 t vanilla
3/4 c sugar
I c carrots, finely grated
2 eggs

Optional:
1/2 c raisins or 1/2 c coconut

Combine mix, baking soda, cinnamon and salt. Make a well in dry ingredients and add nuts, oil, vanilla, sugar, carrots and eggs. Mix just to moisten all ingredients. Fill buttered muffin tins two-thirds full. Bake at 350° for 25 minutes.

Homemade Biscuit Mix

9 c sifted flour
3 T baking powder
2-1/2 t salt
1-1/2 c shortening

Combine dry ingredients. Cut in shortening. Use 2/3 cups milk with 2 cups mix for biscuit dough.

Nippy Carrot Nibblers

Yield: 8 to 12 servings

1 lb. carrots, cut in strips 3" long and 1/4" square
3 T salad oil
3 cloves garlic, minced
1 T onion, coarsely chopped
1/4 c vinegar
1-1/2 t salt
1/2 t dry mustard
1 T whole pickling spices
1/8 t pepper
1 onion, thinly sliced

Prepare recipe the day before or several days ahead.

In skillet, sauté garlic and chopped onion in salad oil until almost tender, about five minutes. Stir in vinegar, salt, mustard, pickling spices tied in cheesecloth, pepper and carrots. Simmer, covered, five minutes; carrots should still be very crunch and crisp. Remove cheesecloth with spices. Transfer carrot mixture to shallow dish; top with layer of thinly sliced onions; cover and refrigerate until needed, basting occasionally. Serve cold as an appetizer, along with shrimp, cherry tomatoes, crisp celery and bunches of green grapes.

Note: The marinade is good for cooked shrimp, too.

Carrot Bread

2 c sifted flour
2 t each baking soda and cinnamon
1/2 t salt
1-1/2 c sugar
1-1/2 c cooking oil
3 eggs
2 t vanilla
2 c carrots, grated
1 c nuts, chopped, or 1 c raisins

In a large bowl sift together the flour, baking soda and cinnamon; add the salt. Make a well in the center and in it put the sugar, cooking oil, eggs and vanilla. With an electric mixer, beat the mixture on medium until well blended. Fold in grated carrots and nuts or raisins. Turn into two well-greased and floured loaf pans and bake in a slow oven 300° for one hour.

Spiced Carrot Cake

    1 t ground cinnamon
    1 t ground mace
    1/2 t salt
    1 c butter or margarine
    2 c sugar
    4 eggs
    1-1/2 c carrots, finely grated
    2/3 c nuts, chopped
    2-1/2 c all purpose flour, sifted
    3 t double-acting baking powder
    1/3 c hot water

Blend spices and salt with butter or margarine. Gradually add sugar, mixing well after each addition. Beat in eggs, one at a time. Stir in carrots and nuts. Sift flour with baking powder and add alternately with water. Beat batter for half a minute. Turn into two well-greased, lightly floured round 9-inch cake pans. Bake in preheated 375°F oven for 35 minutes or until done.

Fill with Fig and Prune Filling.

Cauliflower
. . . .

❖ Soak one-inch cauliflower pieces in salt water (2 tablespoons to 1 gallon water) for 15 minutes to remove insects. Scald each pound cauliflower in 1 gallon boiling water for three minutes. Drip into ice water for three minutes; package and freeze. To serve, boil in small amount of salted water, covered, until tender (about 10 minutes).

Ideas for serving:

Melt 1/4 cup butter. Add 2 tablespoons lemon juice. Pour over hot cauliflower. Add parsley for color.

Use in chow mein, chow fun or other island vegetable dishes. Use raw, thin slices in tossed salads.

Hamburger Supreme

Yield: 5 to 6 servings

    2 lb. hamburger or ground chuck
    salt and pepper to taste
    dash of MSG
    1 medium onion, chopped
    1 clove garlic, minced
    1 4 oz. can mushrooms
    1 can cream of tomato soup
    1 can cream-style corn
    1 pkg. fresh chop suey vegetables (including cauliflower, carrots,
        broccoli and green beans)
    1 pkg. noodles, cooked

Fry in electric fry pan the hamburger with salt, pepper, MSG, onion and garlic until hamburger is browned. Add mushrooms, tomato soup and cream-style corn, mixing thoroughly. Sprinkle chop suey vegetables over top of hamburger. Cover and let simmer for about 10 minutes. Spread one layer of cooked noodles over vegetables. Cover and heat thoroughly. Serve from skillet. This dish may be prepared in a baking pan covered with foil and baked in a 350°F oven until ready to serve.

PICKLED CAULIFLOWER

3 medium-size cauliflower
2 c vinegar
3 c sugar
I c water
1/3 c salt

Soak cauliflower in salted water 10 minutes to remove any bugs. Break into flowerets, then slice 1/8-inch thick. Pack tightly in quart jars. Combine vinegar, sugar, salt and water. Bring to a boil and pour over sliced cauliflower.

CAULIFLOWER, WATER CHESTNUTS AND MUSHROOMS

Yield: 4 servings

1/2 lb. cauliflower
6 water chestnuts
5 dried mushrooms
3 T oil
1/2 c mushroom water
1/4 c cauliflower water
6 dried shrimps
I t sherry
2 T shoyu
I t salt
2 t cornstarch
I t sesame oil

Break cauliflower into flowerets and cut each floweret in two lengthwise. Parboil 1-1/2 minutes in 2 cups boiling water. Reserve 1/4 cup water. Peel water chestnuts and slice. Soak mushrooms and clean. Squeeze dry and slice. Save 1/2 cup of water. Soak shrimps in cauliflower water. Heat pan, add oil, and sauté water chestnuts and mushrooms one minute. Add mushroom and cauliflower water, sherry, shoyu, salt, cornstarch and sesame oil. Simmer half a minute. Add cauliflower and simmer one minute. Garnish with sliced ham.

A 7-oz. can of mushrooms may be substituted for dried mushrooms.

Coconut

❖ Coconut freezes well in all forms—chunks, grated, or the milk.
Calories: 1 cup grated— 306

Coconut Milk

Yield: 2 cups (8 cups coconut milk equals 4 coconuts)

Pour 2 cups boiling liquid (coconut water, water, or milk) over 4 cups grated fresh coconut. Let stand 20 minutes. Strain through poi cloth or a double thickness of cheesecloth, pressing to remove liquid. If coconut milk is heated, bring just to scalding point, stirring constantly to avoid curdling.

Calories: 1/2 cup—252

Coconut Milk (From Packaged Coconut)

Yield: 1 cup

Combine 1-1/3 cup each packaged flaked coconut and cold milk. Refrigerate one hour. Blend for four seconds in blender. Strain.

Beverages

Combine coconut milk with any other island fruit juice for a new treat.

Coconut Cream

Skim top from coconut milk which has chilled in the refrigerator several hours. Six cups of coconut yield 2 cups of cream. Serve plain or whipped.

Calories: 1/2 cup—346

Fresh Coconut Milk (Blender Style)

Cut fresh coconut meat in 1/2-inch cubes. Add 3/4 cup hot liquid for each cup cubes. Blend on high speed 20 to 30 seconds. Let stand 20 minutes. Strain through double thickness of cheesecloth, squeezing out liquid. One coconut gives 1-1/2 to 2 cups.

Coconut Syrup

I c coconut water
3 c fresh coconut, grated
1-1/2 c sugar
1/4 t cream of tartar

Pour the coconut water over the grated fresh coconut. Work with the hands to extract milk from the coconut. When well mixed, strain through a cloth. Take 3/4 cup of the coconut milk and mix with the sugar and cream of tartar. Stir until the sugar is dissolved. Without stirring, cook slowly until syrup drops from the spoon—almost the jelly test. Add half of the remaining liquid and continue cooking until the syrup gives the same test. Then add the remaining liquid and cook again until the syrup drops from the spoon (224°F). Remove from heat and pour into a sterilized jar or cool and beat thoroughly. If poured directly into the jar, the syrup remains transparent, but must be stirred before using to mix the oil which rises to the top. If the syrup is beaten, it becomes thick and milk white. (Courtesy of the University of Hawai'i Agricultural Extension Service.)

Coconut Cream Pie

2 c fresh milk
1/2 c sugar
3 egg yolks, well beaten
1/8 t salt
4 t gelatin
1/4 c cold water
1 t vanilla
2 c grated coconut, well packed
3 egg whites beaten with 2 T sugar
1 9" pie shell, baked
whipped cream
shredded coconut for topping

Combine milk and sugar. Heat to boiling point. Gradually pour half the hot milk mixture into beaten egg yolks, beating constantly. Return egg yolk and milk mixture to saucepan with remaining milk. Add salt and heat back to boiling point. Remove from heat and add gelatin softened in water. Add vanilla and chill until thickened. Add coconut, then fold in beaten egg whites. Fill baked pie shell and chill several hours or overnight. Top with sweetened whipped cream and additional coconut.

Budin (Dessert) (Cora Domingo)

1 c sugar
1/3 c water
5 eggs
1/2 c sugar
1 c diluted cream
1 t vanilla or lemon extract
2 c fruit cocktail, drained
1 c young coconut meat, grated
1/2 contents of small box raisins
1 slice of bread
2 T butter, melted

Cook 1 cup sugar and water together for thick syrup. Beat the eggs, add the cream and 1/2 cup sugar; add vanilla or lemon extract. Line the bottom of pan with thick syrup. Arrange the coconut meat, fruit cocktail and raisins at the bottom of the pan. Pour egg mixture over fruits. Place the slice of bread on top; pour butter over bread.

Fill big pot one-third full of water. Place a rack in the pot and on it place the pan. Cover the pot and bring it to a boil. When the water boils, reduce the temperature to medium and steam until it is dry on top. When mixture is firm and pulls from side of pan, Budin is cooked. Remove from pot and brown under broiler unit. Remove from oven, let stand for a while, then transfer to a platter or large dessert dish. Chill before serving.

Dodol (Filipino Cornstarch Cake)

6 c coconut milk
1 c sugar
1 c cornstarch
2 T vanilla
2 t salt

Mix together coconut milk, sugar, cornstarch and salt in mixing bowl. Stir with a wooden spoon. Cook in saucepan over medium heat for 20 minutes or until pasty and smooth, stirring frequently to prevent lumps. Add vanilla and stir. When done, pour recipe in a baking pan, smoothing the top. Let cool or place in refrigerator. Cut the cake in one-inch squares and serve.

Haupia with Fruit

Yield: 10 to 12 servings

1-1/2 c commercial coconut milk
1-1/2 c water
1/2 c plus 2 T sugar
1/2 c plus 2 T cornstarch
1 c crushed pineapple, peach slices or mango slices

Combine cornstarch, sugar, coconut milk and water. Stir until smooth. Stir over medium heat until thickened. Lower heat and continue cooking for 10 minutes. Pour half into flat pan; spread fruit evenly then pour remaining haupia. Refrigerate until set. Cut into 1-1/2-inch squares.

Fruit may be omitted, if desired.

No-Roll Coconut Crust

Yield: Makes 8-inch pie

1-1/3 c flaked coconut—canned, frozen or fresh
2 T butter or margarine, melted
1/4 c graham cracker crumbs
2 T sugar

Combine coconut and butter; mix well. Add crumbs and sugar, mixing thoroughly. Press firmly on bottom and sides of 8-inch pie pan. Bake in 375°F oven 10 to 12 minutes or until lightly browned. Cool. Fill with softened ice cream and freeze, or other favorite filling. (We use Crystal Passion Fruit Pie Filling.)

Boiled Cookies

Put in saucepan:
1/2 c oleo or butter
2 c sugar
1/3 c cocoa
1/2 c evaporated milk
1/2 t salt
1 t vanilla

Boil two minutes, remove from heat and add:

3 c quick cooking oats
I c coconut, chopped (or peanut butter)
1/2 c nuts, chopped

Drop on waxed paper by teaspoonful. Chill and keep refrigerated.

COCONUT COOKIES

I lb. oleomargarine
2 c sugar
3 c fresh coconut, grated
4 c flour, unsifted

Combine and shape into four rolls as long as waxed paper is wide. Freeze. Remove from freezer; thaw three to four minutes, slice 3/16-inch wide (about 40 cookies per roll). Bake on ungreased cookie sheet at 275°F until golden (about 25 minutes).

FRESH COCONUT CAKE

3/4 c butter
2 c sugar
3 c cake flour, sifted
3 t double-acting baking powder
3/4 c coconut milk
1/4 c water or fresh milk
I t vanilla
I c coconut, freshly grated
1/2 t salt
6 egg whites

Combine butter and sugar until very fluffy. Add flour sifted with baking powder alternately with coconut milk and water, beginning and ending with flour. Add flavoring and grated coconut. Add salt to egg whites and beat until stiff but not too dry. Fold carefully into batter. Pour into three greased and floured 8-inch cake pans. Bake approximately 30 minutes in 350°F oven. Remove from oven and turn onto a cake rack to cool. Frost with fluffy white cooked frosting and pile additional fresh grated coconut on top.

HAUPIA CAKE

1/2 c margarine or butter
I c granulated sugar
2 whole eggs or 2 egg yolks and I whole egg
1-1/2 c cake flour
3 t baking powder
1/4 t salt
1/2 c coconut milk
I t vanilla or lemon extract

Haupia Filling:
I pint coconut milk (2 cups)

1/2 c sugar
6 T cornstarch
1/2 c water
1/4 t salt
1 t vanilla

Frosting:
2 egg whites
1/2 c white corn syrup
1 c coconut, grated

Cream butter and sugar until very light and fluffy. Add eggs and beat again until fluffy. Sift flour, measure, then sift with baking powder and salt. Add dry ingredients alternately with 1/2 cup coconut milk and extract, starting and ending with dry ingredients. Pour into two oiled 8-inch cake pans. Bake 20 minutes at 350°F. Remove cake from pans after cooling for 10 minutes and cool on racks.

Make filling by heating coconut milk to boiling point, then adding sugar, cornstarch that has been dissolved in water, and salt. Stir over medium heat until thick. Add vanilla and cool. Use half on bottom layer and half on top layer of cake. Chill until set.

Top with frosting made by beating egg whites until stiff, and gradually adding syrup while beating until frosting holds its peak. Spread on cake and sprinkle with 1 cup freshly grated or frozen coconut.

CANDIED COCONUT

1 coconut, sliced with vegetable peeler
3/4 or 1/2 c water
1-1/2 c sugar

Double recipe:
3 coconuts
1 c water
3 c sugar

Cook 45 minutes to one hour.
Cook all together until dry on high heat, stirring occasionally (20 minutes).

COCONUT CRUNCH APPLE PIE

Yield: One 9-inch pie

1/2 c sugar
1/4 c brown sugar
2 T flour
1/4 t cinnamon
1/4 t nutmeg
1 9" pie shell, unbaked
4 c apples, sliced
2 T butter or margarine
2 c coconut, shredded

I egg, beaten
1/2 c sugar
1/4 c milk
1/2 t salt

Combine sugars, flour and spices. Into the pie shell place half of the apples; sprinkle with half of spice mixture; repeat with remaining apples and remaining spice mixture. Dot with butter. Cut a double circle of aluminum foil to cover filling only. Bake at 375°F for 30 minutes. Remove foil. Cover with topping made by combining remaining ingredients. Return to oven for 30 minutes.

SALTED COCONUT CHIPS

Slice coconuts with vegetable peeler. It is not necessary to peel off brown outside skin. Put sliced coconut in flat pans and add salt to taste (about 2 tablespoons salt to a coconut). Mix well with hands to be sure each chip is salted. Dry chips in sun or low oven for four to six hours. Toast in 300° oven, turning frequently and watching carefully, until toasted as brown as desired. Remove from oven and separate chips on large dish towels and cool. Store in air-right containers. Makes wonderful pupu.

Cucumbers

❖ Cucumbers cannot be frozen successfully.

Hint: Islanders take the bitterness out of cucumber by slicing off end, then rubbing the end briskly over the slice. A white substance will foam out. Salt may be rubbed on to hurry this. It seems to work because I have **never** had a bitter cucumber when using this method.

CUCUMBER NAMASU (SALAD)

4 medium-size cucumbers
1-1/2 T salt
I can Hokkigai (clams), cut in small pieces
1/2 c sugar
1/2 t salt
1/4 t MSG
1/2 c Japanese vinegar
I t ginger, chopped

Slice cucumbers and sprinkle with 1-1/2 tablespoons salt. Let stand 20 minutes. Drain, press out excess water. Do not rinse. Meanwhile, measure sugar, 1/2 teaspoon salt and MSG into bowl. Add vinegar, ginger and mix well until sugar is dissolved. Add clams, clam juice, and cucumbers. Toss well and chill. Abalone (one-half can) may be used instead of clams.

Variations: soaked, cooked long rice may be added. Sliced celery and carrots may be added.

SWEET PICKLE CHIPS

Use 14 six-inch cucumbers. Wash and place in deep container. Cover with boiling water (no salt). Repeat for three days. On fifth day, drain and slice into 1/4-inch slices.

Combine 1 quart vinegar, 2 cups sugar, 2 tablespoons salt and 2 tablespoons whole pickling spice in cheesecloth bag. Boil and pour over slices. Repeat for four days. On ninth morning, let stand in hot syrup and bring back to a good boil while packing pickles in a jar. Cover with boiling syrup and seal.

EGG FLOWER SOUP WITH CUCUMBER

Yield: 1-1/2 quarts or 4 servings

1/4 lb. lean pork
1-1/2 t sherry
1-1/2 t shoyu
1-1/2 t cornstarch
2 T oil
1-1/2 quart chicken broth
1 green onion, sliced
1 cucumber, sliced
1/4 t MSG
1 t salt
dash of pepper
1 egg, slightly beaten

Cut pork in shreds. Combine sherry, shoyu and cornstarch and mix thoroughly with pork. Heat oil in a deep kettle and quickly brown pork. Add broth and simmer 10 minutes. Add onion, cucumber, MSG, salt and pepper and simmer five minutes more. Bring to a fast boil and slowly add beaten egg, stirring constantly. To be sure that the egg will cook in shreds, or "petals," turn off the heat the moment you add it.

CUCUMBER SUMISO

2 large cucumbers
1 T salt
2 T roasted peanuts, ground, or 2 T sesame seeds
3 T miso
1/2 t MSG
3 T sugar
3 T vinegar
1 T clam juice
1 T mirin
1 t ginger, chopped
2 T green onion, chopped
1 can hokkigai (boiled clams), sliced

Peel cucumbers and cut in half lengthwise. Remove seeds. Slice 1/8-inch thick. Salt and let stand 10 to 15 minutes. Rinse and press out excess water. Make sumiso (vinegar-miso) by combining peanuts, miso, MSG, sugar, vinegar, clam juice, mirin and ginger. Toss onions, cucumber, sliced clams and sumiso together. Chill and serve.

Chinese Cucumbers (Mrs. Pak Wong)

Yield: 4 servings

2 cucumbers (1-1/2 lb.)
1 T cornstarch
2 T shoyu
1/2 t salt
2 t sesame seeds
1 t MSG
2 c water
2 t oil

Peel cucumbers and cut lengthwise into halves. Combine all other ingredients and bring to a boil. Add cucumbers and simmer 15 minutes. Remove cucumbers, slice in 1/2-inch slices, return to gravy.

Pickled Cucumber (1 gallon)

6–7 cucumbers
6 c hot water
1/2 c or less Hawaiian salt
1 c sugar
2 T vinegar
1 t MSG

Halve cucumbers, remove seeds. Slice 3/8-inch thick. Place in clean gallon jar. Combine remaining ingredients. Pour over cucumbers. Refrigerate overnight before eating. Will keep indefinitely.

Mustard Pickles (1 gallon)

6–8 large cucumbers, peeled and sliced
4 onions, diced
6 stalks celery, sliced
2 heads cauliflower, broken finely
2 green peppers, diced
2 sweet red peppers, diced
1/2 c salt
1 gal. water
1 qt. vinegar
4 c sugar
1/2 c plus 1 T flour
1 T celery seed
2 T ground mustard
1 t turmeric

Soak vegetables in salted water overnight. Next morning, rinse and drain. Combine remaining ingredients. Bring to a boil and cook 10 to 15 minutes according to desired crispness. Pour into sterilized jars and seal with tight lids. Keep refrigerated.

Daikon

A member of the turnip family, this long white root has many uses. Boil it like a turnip; slice it like a radish; shred it as a bed for sashimi.

❖ Freeze to be used as a cooked vegetable later. Cut in 1/2-inch cubes. Scald for one minute in boiling water, then dip in ice water for one minute. Package and freeze.

Add to soup, stew, spareribs, or shoyu dishes for just a few minutes before serving.

Hint: That odor from daikon in the refrigerator can be prevented by placing a sheet of plastic wrap between jar and lid.

TAKUAN

1 gal. small whole or sliced daikon
1/4 c Hawaiian salt
1/2 c vinegar
2 c white sugar
2 t yellow coloring

BUTTER YAKI WITH DAIKON SAUCE

Tender beef, sliced very thin (1/2 lb. per person)
1 can Japanese mushrooms, sliced lengthwise
2 medium-size round onions, sliced
1 bunch watercress, cut in 3" lengths
1/2 c butter

Fry above ingredients in butter. Dip in sauce and eat while hot. Have everyone cook own beef and vegetables—four people to a fry pan. Use individual sauce bowls.

Sauce:
1 c shoyu
1/2 c sugar
1/4 c mirin (sweet rice wine)
1/3 c lime juice
2 T sesame seeds, toasted and ground
1/4 t MSG
3/4 c grated daikon

Heat shoyu and sugar until sugar is dissolved. Add mirin, sesame seeds, lime juice and MSG. Add daikon before serving. Leftover sauce may be frozen in jars.

GOOD PUPU IDEA

Cut namasu vegetables (cucumber, daikon and hasu) and abalone in cubes. Soak in regular namasu sauce, then thread on cocktail picks.

Eggplant

❖ Peel and slice in 1/3 to 1/2-inch slices. Scald in boiling water for four minutes. Dip immediately in ice water for three to four minutes. Package and freeze.

Broiled Eggplants (Filipino)

8 medium-size eggplants
3 large eggs
1 t salt
1 t MSG
1/2 c shortening
2 T bread crumbs

Broil eggplants (may be done over charcoal). Remove skin and slice. Heat about 2 tablespoons fat in frying pan. Beat eggs; add salt, MSG and bread crumbs. Dip eggplants in the egg mixture, being sure to cover the eggplants. Fry in hot fat for about two minutes, turning once. Add fat to the pan and continue frying the rest of the eggplants. Serve hot.

Wilted Eggplant with Shoyu (Good pupu)

5 long eggplants
1 T salt
3 T shoyu
1/2 t MSG

Cut eggplants crosswise (slant) in 1/4-inch slices. Salt and let stand 15 minutes. Rinse and press water out. Add shoyu and MSG and serve immediately. This will discolor if left too long in the air.

Broiled Eggplant

Choose uniform eggplants. Place under broiler unit or on charcoal fire. Cook 10 minutes on each side. Eat with shoyu and MSG.

Eggplant Omelet

3 large, long eggplants
1 small onion, chopped fine
1 small tomato, diced
1 T butter or oil
1 T shoyu
1 t salt
2 eggs

Broil eggplants until done (two minutes); peel and dice. Boil onion and tomato in small amount of water until tender. Add butter, shoyu and salt. Combine eggplant with seasoned onions and tomatoes. Beat eggs, pour over vegetables and scramble in oiled fry pan.

Mousakka (Greek) (Eggplant with meat sauce and grated cheese)

2 large eggplants
2 lb. ground round
2 onions, chopped
1 can solid pack tomatoes OR 2 raw tomatoes
1 small can tomato sauce
2 T ketchup

5 eggs
1/4 c flour
1/4 c Parmesan cheese, grated, and
1/2 c Cheddar cheese
parsley, chopped
salt and pepper, sugar and cinnamon
oil for frying

Prepare batter for frying eggplant by beating three eggs with the flour. Fry sliced eggplant, dipped in batter. Brown ground round in a little butter, add chopped onions, tomatoes, sauce, ketchup, parsley, salt, pepper, a pinch of sugar and a pinch of cinnamon. Stir slightly and cook until almost done. Place in a long or square baking pan a layer of eggplant, then a layer of meat sauce, sprinkle generously with grated cheese, cover with another layer of eggplant. Use as many layers as you want but always end with eggplant. Over last layer pour two beaten eggs and sprinkle generously with grated cheese. Bake in a moderate oven until bubbly—about 45 minutes.

Eggplant and Dried Shrimps

1/4 c dried shrimps
3/4 c water
3 T shoyu
1/2 t salt
1/4 t MSG
1 small tomato, chopped
3 eggplants, cut in 1/2" slices

Boil shrimps in covered pan with water for 20 minutes. Add seasonings, chopped tomato and eggplants. Cook until tender, about 10 minutes.

Stuffed Eggplant

2 medium-size oval eggplants
2 T margarine
1 medium onion, chopped
1 T green pepper
1 clove garlic, minced
1 c whole kernel corn
1 can crab meat or tuna
1 egg, slightly beaten
grated cheese

Cut eggplants in half, scoop out insides and dice. Parboil diced pieces in salted water for 15 minutes. Sauté onion, green pepper and garlic in margarine. Add corn, crab meat, diced eggplant and egg. Mix well. Fill eggplant shells with mixture, top with grated cheese. Bake at 350 to 375°F for 35 minutes.

Ginger

❖ Freeze ginger root in small one-inch pieces in heavy plastic bag or sealed container. When ready to use, remove from container and use as if fresh. To use ginger in island recipes—scrape or peel off skin, cut in half and mash with wide, flat knife. Place knife on ginger, the hand on top of knife. One press will mash it OR use garlic press.

Grow ginger shoots to use in cooking. When root begins to look old, plant it in sand in a cool place. New shoots will sprout and can be used for flavoring.

CANDIED GINGER

Peel young ginger root. Cut slanting or crosswise in thin strips. Measure 1 cup ginger to 1-1/2 cups water (cover with water), boil five minutes, drain, and repeat at least four times, depending on strength of the ginger you desire. After the last boiling, measure cooked ginger and water. For each cup of ginger, use 1-1/2 cups sugar.

Boil again until ginger is clear; drain but save the syrup, as it has many uses. Roll drained ginger pieces in granulated sugar. This will keep in a closed container for about a month. Refrigerate for longer storage. Use ginger syrup in hekka, fruit juices, etc.

HAOLE HEKKA

Yield: 4 servings

1 lb. beef, chopped
1 lb. pork, chopped
1 t salt
1/2 t MSG
1/2 c shoyu
2 T bourbon or wine
1/4 c sugar
1 t bottled ginger juice or 1" piece chopped ginger or 1/2 t
    powdered ginger
1 large clove garlic, pressed
1 large round onion, sliced
1 pkg. mixed vegetables
(Include: green beans, carrots, celery and cauliflower)
1/2 pkg. bean sprouts

Fry pork in electric fry pan until well done. Add beef and cook until browned. Add salt, MSG, shoyu, bourbon, sugar, ginger and garlic. Stir to combine ingredients. Cover and simmer while preparing vegetables. (Add water if liquid evaporates too soon.) Slice onion and add to meat. Let cook about one minute, covered. Rinse pre-cut vegetables, drain and add to mixture. Stir to flavor vegetables. Cover and cook about two minutes. Add bean sprouts, stir and cook one minute longer. Serve hot right from skillet. Serve hot rice and fruit with this dish.

TERIYAKI SAUCE

1–1-1/2 lb. sliced beef or chicken
1/2 c shoyu
1/2 c sugar, or less, according to taste
1/4 t MSG

2 T mirin or wine
1 clove garlic, crushed
1" piece ginger, crushed

Combine ingredients and let beef or chicken soak for at least two hours. Broil in oven or over charcoal.

Variations: 2 tablespoons miso may be added for a richer sauce. For a Korean-style sauce, add 2 tablespoons sesame seed oil, 1 teaspoon sesame seeds, 1/4 cup chopped green onions, chili pepper.

JIFFY FISH (CHINESE)

Yield: 4 to 6 servings

6 c water
1-1/2" piece ginger root
1-1/2 T rock salt
2–3 lb. opakapaka
2 T toasted sesame seeds
4 t peanut oil
1/4 c shoyu
dash black pepper
dash MSG
1/2 c green onions, chopped fine

Bring water with ginger and salt added to a boil. Gently lower fish into water. Cook six minutes on one side, turn, cook six minutes on other side. While this is cooking, make sauce by grinding sesame seeds in blender or pounding with knife handle. Put seeds in small pan, then add oil, shoyu, pepper, and MSG. Heat but do not boil. Arrange fish on serving platter, pour sauce over all of fish and garnish with green onions. Serve hot.

Gobo (Burdock)

This is the long, thin, brown root found in the vegetable section of your market. It has a fibrous texture and is used for its texture in island foods.

❖ Prepare by paring off skin with vegetable peeler or scraping with knife. Slice in desired pieces. Scald in boiling water for three minutes, then plunge into ice water to cool. Package and freeze. Gobo cooked in shoyu may also be frozen.

KIMPIRA GOBO

1/2 lb. gobo, scraped
1 doz. dried shrimp
1 T oil
1 chili pepper
2 T sugar
3 T shoyu
1/2 t MSG

Shave gobo into long, narrow pieces and soak in plain water one-half hour. Sauté shrimp and gobo in oil for five to 10 minutes. Add chili pepper, sugar, shoyu and MSG.

Nishime (Japanese)

- 1/2 lb. pork, cut up
- 2 strips nishime konbu
- 3 pieces dried mushrooms (soaked, washed and cut in 1" pieces)
- 2 konyaku, sliced
- 3 aburage (fried tofu), cut in 1" pieces
- 1 c daikon (turnip), cut in stew pieces
- 2 c araimo (Japanese taro), cut in 1/2" pieces
- 1 c carrots, cut in stew pieces
- 1 c gobo (burdock), cut in 1/4" thick diagonal slices and soaked in water until used)
- 2 T oil
- 1-1/2 c water
- 1/2 c shoyu
- 1/3 c sugar
- 1/2 t salt
- 1 t MSG

Soak konbu and mushrooms in water for 10 minutes or until soft. Wash and strip konbu down center, lengthwise, if too wide (more than three inches). Tie in knots about two inches apart. Cut between knots. Fry pork in oil until light brown. Add water, mushrooms, aburage and konbu. Cover; cook for 10 minutes. Add seasoning and cook for five minutes. Add daikon, carrots and gobo; cook for 15 minutes. Add taro and cook until taro is done (about 15 minutes). Stir frequently and do not over-cook as taro will be mushy and nishime will look messy.

Dried shrimps, beef or chicken may be used instead of pork. If hasu (lotus root) is in season, add 1 cup of sliced hasu when adding vegetables.

Guava

Three types—all excellent sources of vitamin C:

Common guava—round, yellow, edible skin surrounding pink or yellow edible pulp and seeds. Can be sweet or tart.

Strawberry guava—small, red and tasting something like a berry. Hawaiian wiwi (vivee).

Pineapple guava—oval-shaped, dull-green color on outside. Center is cream-colored and much sweeter than common guava.

❖ To make purée, put 1/4 cup water in blender. Add quartered guavas until container is three-fourths full. Cover and blend one-half minute. Strain to remove seeds. This pulp may be frozen as is to be used later in these recipes or diluted for juice.

Calories: One medium—30

Juice may be made of either the raw purée by blending it with sugar, water and red food coloring or with the cooked juice as prepared for jelly making. This cooked juice usually needs orange or pineapple juice to improve the flavor. Combine the cooked juice with orange or grape base to add vitamin C and tartness to the bases.

Guava Tapioca

1/4 c minute tapioca
1 c sugar
1/8 t salt
1 c water
1 T lemon juice, if desired
1 t lemon rind, grated
1 c unsweetened fresh guava juice
1/2 c guava shells, thinly sliced

Combine tapioca, sugar, salt and water. Cook slowly over direct heat until tapioca is clear (about five minutes). Remove from range and stir in remaining ingredients. Pour into individual dishes or serving bowls and chill. Serve with thin cream or whipped cream.

Guava Ice Box Cake

8 lady fingers
1 T gelatin
1/4 c cold water
1/3 c sugar
1/4 c boiling water
1 can frozen guava concentrate
2 egg whites
1/8 t salt
1/2 c whipping cream (optional)

Line a mold with halves of lady fingers. Soak gelatin in cold water until softened. Add gelatin and sugar to boiling water. Stir until dissolved. Cool and add concentrate. Mix thoroughly and place in refrigerator to congeal. When partially set, beat egg whites with salt until soft peaks hold. Whip gelatin mixture, then fold in egg whites. Pour into prepared mold. Chill four to six hours. Turn out on plate and garnish with whipped cream.

Variation: Use thin slices of sponge cake instead of lady fingers. Use 1/2 cup fresh pulp and increase sugar to 1 cup.

Guava Chiffon Pie

4 egg yolks
1/2 c frozen guava concentrate
1/4 c sugar
1/4 t salt
1 pkg. gelatin
1/4 c water
1 T lemon juice
3/4 c frozen guava concentrate
4 egg whites
1/4 c sugar

Separate eggs. Beat egg yolks until light. Add 1/4 cup sugar, 1/4 teaspoon salt and 1/2 cup guava concentrate.

Cook mixture in top of double boiler until smooth and thickened slightly, stirring continually. Soak gelatin in water to soften and add to hot mixture. Remove and cool to room temperature. Add lemon juice and remainder of guava concentrate. Chill until partly set.

Whip egg whites until stiffened. Add sugar slowly while continually beating. Whip partly set gelatin mixture and fold in egg whites. Pour into pie shell and top with whipped cream.

HAWAIIAN HARVEST CAKE

I c white sugar
I c brown sugar
1/2 c shortening
2 eggs
2-1/2 c flour, unsifted
I t soda
1/2 t salt
I c milk
I c fresh or frozen guava pulp

Topping:
1/3 c brown sugar
1/3 c butter
1/2 c coconut, grated
1/2 c nuts, chopped

Cream sugars and shortening, add eggs. Mix in flour, soda and salt along with milk and guava pulp. Beat only until smooth. Pour into greased 13x9x2-inch baking pan. Sprinkle topping over batter. Bake in 350°F oven for 50 minutes.

FRESH GUAVA CHIFFON PIE

I pie shell, baked
I T unflavored gelatin
1/4 c water
I c sugar
2/3 c guava pulp, strained (unsweetened)
4 egg yolks
3–4 T lemon or lime juice
1/4 c guava juice
4 egg whites
1/8 t salt
1/2 c sweetened whipped cream, if desired

Sprinkle gelatin over cold water and let stand five minutes. Combine 1/2 cup sugar, guava pulp and egg yolks. Beat until well mixed. Cook over hot water, stirring constantly, until it thickens. Add gelatin, remove from heat and stir until thoroughly combined. Cool and add fruit juice.

When guava mixture begins to congeal, beat egg whites and salt until stiff; add 1/2 cup sugar and beat until glossy. Gently fold guava mixture into beaten egg whites, pour into pie shell, and place in refrigerator to chill. Before serving, filling may be spread with whipped cream sweetened to taste.

Guava Chiffon Cake

Yield: One 10-inch cake

2-1/4 c cake flour
1-1/2 c sugar
3 t baking powder
1 t salt
1/2 c salad oil
5 egg yolks
3/4 c guava juice
2 t vanilla
1 t lemon rind, grated
1/2 c guava pulp
1 c egg whites
1/2 t cream of tartar

Sift flour, sugar, baking powder and salt in mixing bowl. Make well in center; add oil, egg yolks, guava juice, vanilla, lemon rind and guava pulp. Beat until smooth. Beat egg whites and cream of tartar until whites form very stiff peaks. Pour yolk mixture gradually over whites, folding gently until blended. Pour into unoiled 10-inch tube pan. Bake at 325°F for 55 minutes. Then at 350°F for 10 minutes.

Guava Frosting

1 egg white
3 T soft butter
2 c powdered sugar, unsifted
1/4 t salt
3 T frozen guava concentrate
1 t vanilla
3–4 drops red coloring

Put the frozen guava concentrate, egg white, vanilla, butter and salt into the blender container. Cover and blend at high speed. Add 1 cup sugar and blend at high speed. Push the ingredients down from the sides of the container with a rubber spatula when necessary. Add remaining sugar and mix thoroughly at high speed.

Rich Guava Filling

1/3 c granulated sugar
1-1/2 T cornstarch
1/8 t salt
1 t lemon rind, grated
1 T lemon juice
5 egg yolks, slightly beaten
3/4 c guava juice
2 T butter or margarine

In double boiler top or heavy saucepan, thoroughly mix sugar, cornstarch and salt. Stir in lemon rind and juice, then rest of ingredients. Cook over boiling water or low heat, stirring constantly, until smooth and thick (about 15 minutes). Refrigerate until cold. Fills two eight-inch or nine-inch layers.

Guava Jelly

Wash and slice slightly underripe guavas. Place in kettle and add water to almost cover. Boil slowly, stirring occasionally, for 30 to 40 minutes. Strain through wet jelly bag or doubled cheesecloth, without squeezing the bag. Taste juice. If not tart, add juice of lemon or one lime. Measure 4 cups juice into large kettle. Boil 8 to 10 minutes, then add 4 cups sugar. Cook rapidly to 222°F on a candy thermometer or until jelly sheets off spoon. Skim and pour into hot sterilized jelly glasses. Seal with paraffin.

Punch (for 80)

1 gal. canned guava nectar
2 large cans pineapple juice
3 cans frozen lilikoi, diluted
6 cans Exchange Orange Base, diluted
2 large bottles ginger ale

Mix juices together. Chill. Add ginger ale just before serving. Float scoops of guava or pineapple sherbet on top.

Guava Jello

1 3 oz. pkg. strawberry gelatin dessert
1 3 oz. pkg. lemon gelatin dessert
2 c boiling water
1 c smooth guava purée
1 c cold water

Pour boiling water over strawberry and lemon gelatin in 9x9-inch square pan. Stir until all gelatin is dissolved. Add guava purée and cold water. Chill until firm.

Guava Bread with Butter Crust Topping

Yield: One loaf

1 c sugar
1/2 c butter
2 eggs
1 t vanilla
2 c sifted flour
1 t cinnamon
1/2 t salt
1 t soda
1 t baking powder
1/4 c sour cream
1 c guava pulp
1/4 c macadamia nuts, chopped

Topping:
1/4 c flour
1/4 c brown sugar
1/4 t salt
4 T butter, chilled
1/2 t cinnamon
1 T orange rind, grated

Cream sugar and butter well. Beat in eggs, one at a time. Add vanilla. Sift together flour, cinnamon, salt, baking soda, baking powder. Combine sour cream and guava pulp and add alternately with dry ingredients. Blend in nuts. Bake in waxed paper lined loaf pan at 350°F for a half hour; sprinkle topping over bread, then bake one-half hour more.

GUAVA CATSUP

Yield: 1 pint

3 c guava pulp
6 T onion, chopped
1 t whole cloves
1 stick cinnamon, 2" long
1 t whole allspice
3/4 c sugar
1/2 c vinegar
1–3 small Hawaiian peppers
1 clove garlic, chopped fine
few drops red coloring

Use freshly sieved or canned guava pulp or that left from juice or jelly making. Tie spices loosely in a small piece of cloth. Combine all ingredients. Cook about two hours or until of catsup consistency, stirring frequently to prevent burning. Strain through a sieve, if desired, and tint with a few drops of red coloring. Again heat to boiling; pour immediately into hot sterilized bottles and seal.

Kamani Nuts

Kamani nuts are edible without being roasted. Simply crack the nut open and eat the slivers of meat.

Kukui Nuts

Kukui nuts are usually roasted before cracking open. They should be roasted in a slow oven (275°F) for two hours. At the end of this time, crack one open and taste to see that the rawness is gone. Roast longer if necessary. Kukui is very laxative, so must be eaten sparingly.

Kumquats

❖ These small oranges are not satisfactory for freezing.

PRESERVED KUMQUATS

1 lb. kumquats
1-1/2 c sugar
4 c water

Wash kumquats in warm, soapy water. Rinse, cover with water and boil for 15 minutes. Drain well and repeat twice. Make syrup of sugar and water by boiling for five minutes. Place drained kumquats in hot syrup and bring to 238°F on a candy thermometer or let boil gently until fruits are transparent. To keep fruit plump, cover pan just before removing from heat and let set covered with syrup 30 minutes. Pack in sterile jars. Serve as garnish for meat and desserts.

CANDIED KUMQUATS

Use the above method, then drain from syrup. With toothpick, put a hole in stem end. Bring to boil a heavier syrup of one part water to one part sugar. Add 1/8 teaspoon cream of tartar for every quart of liquid. Re-boil fruit for 30 minutes in this syrup. Remove from heat, but allow kumquats to stand in this syrup for 24 hours. Bring to boil again; cook 30 minutes more. Drain, dry on rack and roll in granulated sugar.

KUMQUAT MARMALADE

Yield: Makes six small jars

3 lb. kumquats
6 c water
4 c sugar

Scoop pulp from skins. Cover skins with cold water and cook until tender. If bitter flavor is not desired, drain and repeat this process at least four times during cooking time, replacing cold water. When tender, grind the skins. Meanwhile, cover the pulp with 3 cups water and simmer for 30 minutes. Strain and add remaining water to juice. Discard pulp and seeds. Add sugar and ground skins. Cook until syrup jells. Pour into hot sterilized jars and seal with melted paraffin.

BAKED CHICKEN WITH KUMQUATS

Yield: 6 servings

5–6 lb. roasting chicken, cut in serving-size pieces
1/2 c dry white wine
1/4 c each lime juice and shoyu
2 small onions, finely chopped (about 1 cup)
4 cloves garlic, crushed
1/2 t each oregano and thyme
1 t each curry powder and ground ginger

2 T butter or margarine
1 T salad oil
2 T flour
1 c halved canned kumquats
2 egg yolks, slightly beaten
salt, to taste
chopped parsley

Place chicken pieces in a large shallow baking dish. Combine wine, lime juice, shoyu, onion, garlic, oregano, thyme, curry and ginger. Pour over chicken, cover and allow to marinate six to eight hours, turning twice. Drain and reserve marinade. Heat butter and oil in large frying pan. Brown chicken and return to the baking dish. Stir flour into the fat remaining in the pan and cook, stirring until bubbly. Gradually stir in marinade and cook until thickened. Pour sauce over chicken, cover with foil, and place in moderate oven (350°F) for one hour, or until tender. Using tongs, remove chicken from sauce and arrange in a shallow serving dish or casserole; reserve sauce. Sprinkle with kumquats and keep warm while you finish sauce.

Pour sauce into a small pan and bring to a boil. Blend some of the hot liquid with egg yolks, then return mixture to pan. Cook, stirring constantly, until sauce is thickened; do not boil. Salt to taste. Pour sauce over chicken. Sprinkle with parsley.

Lemons

❖ Lemon slices may be frozen in decorative ice molds. Lemon rind may be stored in small chunks in plastic bag. (Make grated lemon rind in blender by putting quarter-size pieces of rind in small mayonnaise jar instead of blender container. Let blender do the grating.) Lemon juice may be frozen in ice trays, then cubes stored in plastic bag.

Uses for lemon:

- Add lemon juice to avocado, banana or artichoke hearts before freezing to prevent discoloration.
- Dip cut apples, peaches, pears and bananas in lemon juice to prevent browning.
- Add lemon to vegetables just before serving to enhance flavor.
- Add a little lemon juice to potatoes as they boil to keep them white.
- Lemon juice can tenderize cuts of meat.
- Add 1 tablespoon lemon juice to 1 cup milk to make sour milk when recipe calls for sour milk.

LEMON MERINGUE PIE FOR THE FREEZER

2-2/3 c sugar
1/2 t salt
1 c cornstarch
3 c hot water
6 egg yolks

2/3 c fresh lemon juice
2 t lemon peel, grated
2 T butter
2 9" pie shells, baked

Mix sugar, salt and cornstarch in pan. Add hot water gradually, cook over direct heat, stirring constantly until thickened and clear (six to eight minutes). Remove from heat. Stir 1/2 cup of hot mixture gradually into beaten egg yolks; stir this back into hot mixture. Cook for six minutes at low heat, stirring constantly. Remove from heat; add lemon juice, grated peel and butter. Cool slightly; pour into cool baked pie shells. Top with meringue according to directions.

MERINGUE FOR PIE BAKED AT ONCE:

3 egg whites
1/4 t cream of tartar
6 T sugar

Beat egg whites and cream of tartar until frothy. Add sugar gradually, beating until meringue holds in firm glossy peaks. Spread meringue on pie. Bake at 400°F (seven to eight minutes) until brown.

MERINGUE FOR FROZEN PIE:

If you use frozen egg whites, thaw to room temperature before beating. Follow directions above, but brown in 350°F oven, 15 to 20 minutes.

LEMON MILKSHAKE

Yield: 2 servings

1 c milk
3 T frozen concentrate for lemon OR 1 T lemon juice and 2 T
    sugar
1 medium banana
1/2 c ice cream
1 c cracked ice

Put milk in blender container, add remaining ingredients. Blend on high-speed one to two minutes.

Limu (Seaweed)

❖ Clean limu, break into small pieces, pour boiling water over it and let stand for one-half minute. Drain, then rinse in cold water. Put in heavy plastic bags and freeze. Use in recipes below.

OPIHI LIMU

Gather and clean limu. Pour boiling water over limu; rinse with cold water after one-half minute. Squeeze and drain. Toss with salted opihi.

Chop Chop Limu

Gather and clean limu; chop in 1/2-inch pieces. Toss with salted opihi.

Limu-Onion Relish

Prepare ogo (limu manauea) as directed above. Add chopped round onions and the following vinegar sauce:

1/2 c sugar
1/2 t salt
1/2 t MSG
1/2 c Japanese vinegar

Cucumber-Seaweed Namasu (Japanese)

3 medium-size cucumbers
3 c prepared limu (limu manauea)
1/2 c sugar
1/2 t salt
1/2 t MSG
1/2 c Japanese vinegar
2 T shoyu
1 t ginger, chopped
1/2 can abalone juice (#1 size)
1/2 can abalone, slivered

Prepare limu by washing thoroughly. Break or cut into small pieces. Pour boiling water over limu. Drain; press water from limu. Slice cucumbers. Sprinkle with salt; let stand 20 minutes. Drain; press out excess water. Meanwhile, measure sugar, salt and MSG in bowl. Add vinegar, shoyu, abalone juice and ginger. Mix well until sugar is dissolved. Add abalone, cucumber and seaweed. Toss well and chill.

Loquat

❖ Loquats resemble small peaches in texture, color and skin fuzziness. They are grown in the Makawao and Kula areas.

Cooked loquat may be frozen. Peel and remove seeds. Cook eight minutes in water almost to cover. Drain off water, cool and pack in sealed container. Fresh loquats can be frozen to be used partially frozen in salads later. Halve and peel loquats. Sprinkle lightly with sugar. Freeze in moisture-proof container.

Loquat Pie

3 c loquats
1/2 t salt
1/2 c granulated sugar
1/2 c light brown powdered sugar (not raw)
4 T tapioca
1 T lemon juice

1/8 t nutmeg
margarine
1/2 t cinnamon
pastry for 9" double crust pie

Line 9-inch pie plate with bottom crust. Peel and remove seeds from loquats. Cook for eight minutes in water (enough to cover fruit). Drain water from cooked fruit. In mixing bowl combine loquats, salt, sugars, tapioca, lemon juice, cinnamon and nutmeg. Stir lightly. Pour mixture into pastry-lined plate. Dot with margarine. Place top crust over filling, trim and seal. Prick to allow for escape of steam. Brush top with milk. Bake in hot oven (425°F) for 10 minutes then lower heat to 350° for 25 minutes.

MRS. YOUNG'S LOQUAT JAM

Yield: About 1-1/2 pints

4 c loquat halves or pieces
3 T lemon juice
3-1/2 c sugar (approximate—see directions)

Wash, peel and seed loquats—place halves or pieces in salted water (1 tablespoon to the quart) as you prepare them. This prevents discoloration until ready for measuring.

Measure prepared fruit (pack it firmly) into a 2-quart kettle. Add lemon juice at once. Place on burner, chopping and stirring with spoon to tear up fruit and start juice flowing. Cook until fruit is tender and liquid is reduced (about 15 minutes). Measure.

Add 1 cup sugar to each cup of cooked fruit, then boil vigorously until mixture reaches jelly stage (about 15 minutes) stirring frequently to prevent scorching.

Remove from heat, stir for a few minutes. Skim to remove foam, then pour into sterilized dry jars that have caps and rings for perfect sealing. Seal at once.

Variation: Use two-thirds loquat and one-third pineapple when measuring the fruit.

Instruction for Canning Loquats

Use plain tin cans or glass jars with self-sealing caps and rings. Use mature but firm fruit. Remove the stem and blossom end of the loquat and peel. Cut in halves, remove seeds (loquats may be canned with seeds left in if desired). Pack the loquats (cold) to within 1/4 inch of the top of jars or cans. Add boiling medium syrup to completely fill the container (1 cup of sugar to 2 cups of water. Add 1 teaspoon lemon juice to each cup of syrup). OR preheat the loquat halves in boiling syrup (boil for about three minutes) then pack them in the container. No exhaust (heating in open container before sealing) is necessary when fruit is preheated and packed hot. If loquats are packed into containers cold and hot syrup added, then exhaust containers of fruit in boiling water for 10 minutes (pints), 12 minutes (quarts). (Center can temperature should be at least 170°F.) When containers are heated as described, seal immediately and do not allow to cool before processing. Process (cook) sealed containers, completely submerged in boiling water, 12 minutes for glass pints, 15 minutes for glass quarts, 12 minutes for No. 2 cans. (Count processing time **after** water comes to a rolling boil.) Cool quickly after processing. Air cool the jars away from drafts. Cool tins in clean cold water. When nearly cold, dry and label. Store in cool, dark, dry place.

LOQUAT JELLY

4 c juice (see instructions)
1 pkg. powdered pectin
5-1/2 c sugar

Wash and stem 5 pounds ripe loquats. Remove seeds. Add 1 cup water and 1/2 cup lemon juice. Simmer, covered, 15 minutes. Squeeze out juice. Measure juice and pour into large kettle. Add pectin and stir well. Place over Hi heat, bring to a boil, stirring constantly. When boil cannot be stirred down, add sugar, mix well. Continue stirring and bring again to a full rolling boil. Then boil exactly two minutes. Remove from heat. Let boil subside, then skim carefully and pour into hot, sterilized glasses. Seal with paraffin.

Lotus Root (Hasu)

This root is a series of brown bulbs. When sliced, it has an elegant, lacy design.
❖ Hasu may be frozen if carefully prepared. Peel and cut in half lengthwise. Plunge into boiling water and remove from heat immediately when water starts to boil again. Cool under running water. Package and freeze. Use in cooked island foods upon defrosting.

HASU SANBAIZUKE

2 c hasu (lotus root) (2 medium bulbs)
2 c daikon
1 c carrots
1 T salt
3/4 c Japanese vinegar
3/4 c sugar
1 t salt
1/2 t MSG
1/2 large lime
1" piece ginger, chopped

Peel hasu and cut in half lengthwise. Plunge hasu into boiling water and remove from heat immediately when water starts to boil again. Cool under running water. Drain; slice thin crosswise. Slice daikon and carrots thin, crosswise. Salt daikon and carrots five minutes, rinse and drain. Press excess water out. Combine vinegar, sugar, MSG, and lime juice. Add hasu, daikon, carrots, and ginger to vinegar sauce.

CANDIED LOTUS ROOT

Yield: Approximately 2-1/2 dozen

2 medium lotus roots, peeled and sliced crosswise,
   1/4" thick

Syrup:
4 c sugar
2 c water
1/4 t vanilla extract
1 c granulated sugar

Place lotus roots in bowl of water to prevent discoloration.

Combine syrup ingredients; bring to a boil and simmer five minutes. Add lotus root; simmer gently five minutes. Lift vegetables from syrup with slotted spoon and arrange in single layer on wire racks over pan to catch drippings. Cover lightly with waxed paper. Save syrup.

Next day reheat syrup to boiling, add vegetables and simmer two minutes. Lift from syrup and return to wire racks. Cover lightly with waxed paper and let stand overnight.

Repeat this cooking and draining process two more times or until vegetables are firm.

Roll in granulated sugar and store in airtight container.

Lychee and Longan

Lychee is a fruit similar in texture to a grape. It has a rough, tough skin and is the size of a small lime. The flavor is unusual, but will grow on you.

Calories: One fruit—12

Longan has the same texture, but is smaller in size with a skin that is smooth.

❖ Freeze whole in shells. Remove from freezer and use immediately or the texture will be unsatisfactory. Peeled lychee may be frozen in a syrup (one part sugar to five parts water) or in whipped cream.

Longan or Lychee combinations

Salad of mixed fruits, including grapefruit, mango, orange, pineapple, and seedless grapes. Make juice if you have an excess of fruit by merely running them through a blender or a sieve. Combine with other island juices, such as lime and/or pineapple. Serve on top ice cream. Add to Chinese dishes in place of pineapple.

GLAZED LYCHEE

4 T sugar
4 T water
12 lychees, peeled and pitted

Put sugar and water in saucepan and boil until syrupy. Add lychees and let soak only one minute. Set aside to cool. Use to trim salads or Chinese pork.

FROZEN PIE

1 pt. (1/2 qt.) vanilla ice cream
1 c whipping cream
2 T sugar
1/4 t salt
1/2 c mango, chopped
1 c lychee, sliced

Cut ice cream in 1/2-inch slices; lay on bottom of pie pan to cover. Cut remaining slices in half; arrange around rim. With tip of spoon, smooth into a crust shape. Freeze until firm. Whip cream, add sugar and salt; fold in mango and lychee. Freeze in ice cream shell.

LYCHEES WITH HAM

Add 1/2 cup peeled and pitted fresh lychees to the top of ham during the last hour of baking. This adds a delicious taste and seems to tenderize and bring out the fullest flavor. The partially baked lychee is tasty.

LYCHEE SALAD

Remove seeds from peeled lychees and stuff with cream cheese which has been thinned with a little cream or mayonnaise. Chopped walnuts, pecans or preserved ginger may be added. Serve on lettuce leaves with mayonnaise to which a little whipped cream has been added.

CALAVO'S DESSERT OF THE GODS

Yield: 6 servings

36 lychees, peeled, pitted and halved
1/4 c brandy
1 c whipping cream
6 shortcakes

Marinate lychees in brandy four to six hours or overnight. Whip cream until very stiff. Fold marinated lychee into cream. Mound on shortcakes.

Variations on this are unlimited. Line a mold with sponge cake, fill with whipped cream and lychees. To make the whipped cream lighter, fold in egg whites beaten with 2 tablespoons sugar. Chill until firm. Cut in serving pieces and garnish with Glazed Lychees.

CHICKEN LYCHEE

Yield: 6 servings

1 3 lb. fryer, boned, sliced thin
1 egg white
1" piece ginger root, minced
1 T cornstarch
4 T shoyu
1 T cornstarch
2 T pineapple syrup or washed sugar
2 T lemon juice or vinegar
1/4 c salad oil
2 c lychee or longan halves
parsley

Mix chicken, egg white, ginger and 1 tablespoon cornstarch. Combine shoyu, 1 tablespoon cornstarch, syrup and lemon juice. Heat heavy skillet, very hot. Add oil and heat. Stir-fry chicken until done, add shoyu mixture and lychees, cook until gravy is slightly thickened and lychees are hot. Garnish with parsley. Serve with hot rice.

Macadamia Nuts

❖ Macadamia nuts freeze very well. This keeps nuts from turning rancid.

Use macadamias in stuffings, all baked goods calling for nuts, in ice cream or salted as a pupu.

Drying and Roasting Macadamia Nuts

Gather nuts and husk as soon as possible; otherwise, mildew can ruin nuts. Hang nuts in basket or bag in dry place for three weeks to six months. When ready to roast, place single layers on cake racks or in pans at 150°F. Put smaller nuts in separate pan. Remove after two hours. Roast larger nuts four hours at 150°F, then increase temperature to 200°F for one hour. Cool and crack. For best cracking results, use a light, easy to handle hammer. Chip a slight indentation in cement or a heavy wooden board. Place nut stem side down in "puka." Hit squarely on flower end. Nuts will usually come out whole. To salt nuts, sauté in butter, then sprinkle with salt. Or you may heat the nuts in a 275°F oven for 10 minutes. Brush with oil, sprinkle with powdered salt. (Put salt through blender.) Or you may soak nuts in salt water overnight and re-dry in a 150°F oven for one hour.

MACADAMIA CREAM PIE

Yield: One 9-inch pie

1/4 c cornstarch
2/3 c sugar
1/4 t salt
2 c milk
3 egg yolks, slightly beaten
1 c macadamia nuts, chopped
2 T butter or margarine
1/2 t vanilla
1 9" pie shell, baked
3 egg whites
1/2 t cream of tartar
6 T sugar

Blend cornstarch, the 2/3 cup sugar, and salt in saucepan. Add milk; cook over low heat, stirring constantly until thick. Thoroughly stir half of hot mixture into egg yolks; then return all to mixture in saucepan. Cook five minutes more, stirring constantly. Add macadamia nuts, butter and vanilla; cool. Pour into baked pie shell. Beat egg whites and cream of tartar until frothy. Gradually add remaining sugar, beating well after each addition. Continue beating until glossy peaks are formed. Swirl meringue over pie; bake at 325°F for 15 minutes or until golden brown. Cool before serving.

Macadamia Bavarian Cream Pie

1 9" or 10" pie shell, baked and cooled
1 envelope unflavored gelatin
1/4 c sugar
1/8 t salt
2 eggs, separated
1-1/4c milk
1/2t vanilla
3/4c macadamia nuts, finely ground
1/4c sugar
1c whipping cream, whipped, or
   2/3 cup icy cold evaporated milk, whipped

Mix gelatin, sugar and salt together thoroughly in top of double boiler or heavy saucepan. Beat together egg yolks and milk; add to gelatin mixture. Cook over boiling water or on medium heat, stirring constantly until gelatin is thoroughly dissolved, about eight minutes. Remove from heat, add vanilla. Chill to unbeaten egg white consistency. Add nuts. Beat egg whites until stiff; beat in 1/4 cup sugar gradually. Fold in gelatin mixture. Fold in whipped cream. Turn into pie shell and chill 12 hours before serving. Top with more macadamia nuts, coconut or whipped cream.

Macadamia Sundae Sauce

Yield: About 3/4 cup

1 T butter
1/2 c unsalted chopped macadamias
1/2 c powdered sugar, unsifted
1/2 c heavy cream
dash of salt

Melt butter in a small frying pan; add macadamias and stir until lightly toasted; this takes about one minute over medium-high heat. Blend in the powdered sugar, then mix in the cream and salt. Boil rapidly, stirring constantly, until sauce is smooth and shiny-looking. Remove from heat. Serve hot or cool. Store, covered, in the refrigerator. To reheat, set container of sauce in hot water.

Hawaiian Fruit Cake

Yield: Two 2-pound loaves or one loaf and 36 small cakes

1-3/4 c raisins
2-1/2 c mixed candied fruit
1/2 c dates, cut in half
3/4 c candied cherries
1-1/4 c macadamia nuts
1-1/4 c coconut, shredded
1-1/3 c enriched flour
1 c brown sugar
2/3 c shortening

4 eggs
1/2 t cinnamon
1/2 t nutmeg
1/2 t cloves
1/2 t soda
1/2 c guava jelly
1 T brandy
1 T sherry
1/2 t ginger juice

Mix fruits and nuts with half the flour. Cream sugar and shortening; beat in eggs. Sift spices and soda with remaining flour; add to creamed mixture. Combine jelly, brandy, sherry and ginger juice with fruit; mix well with batter. Pour into oiled and waxed-paper lined pans. Bake at 275°F for three hours.

Bake small cakes one hour at 275°F.

GLAZE FOR FRUIT CAKES

1 c syrup
1 c water

Cook until mixture forms soft ball in cold water or until it reaches 238°F on a candy thermometer. Brush hot syrup over fruit cakes. Arrange decorations on cake. Brush again with syrup. Place in 350°F oven for 10 minutes.

MARY OH'S PIE CRUST

1 block butter, semi-melted
1 c flour
1/2 c macadamia chips
1/2 c brown sugar

Mix butter and flour. Add nuts and brown sugar. Put in buttered pie plate. Bake at 450°F for 15 minutes, stirring every five minutes. Remove from oven and shape with spoon. Refrigerate.

Filling:
1 c whipping cream
1 8 oz. pkg. cream cheese
1/2 t vanilla
3/4 c powdered sugar
1 can cherry or blueberry pie filling, chilled

Whip cream. Cream the cheese with vanilla and powdered sugar. Fold in whipped cream. Pour into chilled pie crust. Top with chilled pie filling and chill several hours before serving.

PEANUT BRITTLE OR MACADAMIA NUT BRITTLE

2 c white sugar
1 c white syrup
1/2 c water
3 c nuts (if macadamia nuts are used, they should be cut into 1/4 nut size)

2 t baking soda
I t vanilla
1/4 stick butter

Have ingredients measured out beforehand; they must be used quickly.

Cook sugar, water and syrup until a long thread is formed by test. Add the nuts to the hot syrup and continue cooking until both the syrup and nuts are a light tan color and the syrup is real bubbly. Remove from heat and add, very quickly, the soda, vanilla and butter. Stir rapidly just long enough to mix well. By this time it will almost overflow from the pan. Pour quickly on a shallow pan that has been buttered. Do not try to spread; it will spread itself. If you try to spread it, you will burst the bubbles that make it so crunchy. Let cool until you can lift it up in one sheet. Turn the sheet of candy over. When cool and hard enough to break, you can break the sheet into pieces the size you want by hitting the sheet with the handle of a knife.

Mango

❖ Slice the flesh from the seed leaving the fibrous part for making mango purée. Either sprinkle mango slices with one part granulated sugar to 10 parts fruit or make a syrup using 1-1/2 cups sugar to 2 cups water. Let the syrup cool before slicing mangoes into it. Fill the containers—plastic boxes, freezer bags or glass jars—to one inch from the top. Food and water expand when frozen. This prevents broken jars and split plastic bags in the freezer.

Scrape the seeds and combine this pulp with odd-size pieces of mango. Put through a sieve to remove stringy portions. Add sugar in the proportion of one part granulated sugar to 8 to 10 parts fruit. When labeling, be sure to mark how much sugar is in each package in case you want to make a mango pulp cake or bread later. You will need to decrease the sugar in the recipe by the amount that is included in the pulp.

Use partially frozen mango slices for salads, shortcakes, ice cream topping, breakfast or snack fruit.

Calories: 1 small—66

MANGO JAM

12 c half-ripe or ripe mango slices
4 c water
6 c sugar

Add water to mango slices and cook about 15 minutes or until tender. Press the mixture through a sieve, add sugar and boil until thick and of proper consistency for a jam. Pour into hot, sterile jars and seal with paraffin.

CANNING MANGO SLICES

Select firm-ripe or half-ripe mangoes that are not fibrous. Peel and slice in large slices. Save remaining pulp for sauce. Prepare a medium syrup by adding 1 cup of sugar to 1 cup of water. Heat. Stir until sugar is dissolved and syrup begins to boil.

Add mango slices to the hot syrup and cook for about 10 minutes. Pack in hot, sterilized jars and cover with boiling syrup to within 1/2 inch of the top of the jar. Seal and process 15 to 20 minutes in water bath (water should come to one to two inches over the top of the jar).

Mango Bread

3 c flour (measure after sifting)
I t soda
1/2 t baking powder
1/4 t salt
2 large eggs
1/2 c shortening or margarine
3/4 c sugar
I c diced, ripe mangoes
I T lemon juice, sprinkle over mangoes
1/2 c chopped nuts, walnuts or pecans

Sift together flour, soda, baking powder and salt. Cream shortening and sugar. Add beaten eggs. Add flour mixture alternately with the juicy mangoes. Fold in chopped nuts. Bake one hour in greased loaf pan at 375°F.

Mango Marmalade

Yield: 2 pints

4 c mango scraps from mango canning
2 T fresh lemon juice
1/4 c slivers of fresh lemon (rind and pulp cut very thin)
3 c granulated sugar

Cook mango "scraps" at low heat for about 25 minutes or until product is mushy and reduced to about 3 cups. Do not add water. Add lemon juice, slivers and sugar. Boil rapidly, stirring constantly, for about 10 minutes or until mixture looks clear and lemon slivers are translucent.

Pour boiling marmalade into sterilized dry jars. Fill to top of jar and seal immediately. Label and store in cool, dry place—preferably dark (to preserve color).

Mango Butter

12 c half-ripe mango, peeled and sliced
3 c water
6 c sugar
1/2 t ground cloves
1/2 t ground allspice
I t ground cinnamon
I t ground nutmeg

Add water to mangoes and cook until soft enough to mash. Press through a sieve if the mangoes are stringy. Add sugar and spices. Cook slowly for 45 minutes or until thick. Stir frequently to prevent burning. Pour into hot sterile glasses and seal with paraffin.

SHREDDED MANGO (PRESERVED)

2 c mango, shredded
salt (Hawaiian salt is best)
I c sugar
I t (or less) Chinese five spice
few drops red food coloring

Sprinkle shredded or sliced mango with salt and let stand overnight. When ready to cook, drain off all liquid. Cook drained mango in sugar, spice and coloring until well sweetened, but still firm.

MANGO SEEDS

I gal. dried mango seeds
2 boxes brown sugar
3/4 t five spice
red coloring
salted lime, minced (optional)
water

In a large pot, add enough water to cover the mango seeds and boil it for one-half hour. Drain and add sugar over slow flame, stirring constantly (one-half hour). Add coloring, spice, and lime and continue cooking for another one-half hour and stirring constantly.

RIPE MANGO PIE

I pie shell, baked
4–5 c ripe mango slices
1/4 c sugar
I t vanilla
2 egg whites
pinch cream of tartar
4 T sugar

Peel and slice mangoes and sprinkle with sugar and vanilla. Add cream of tartar to egg whites and beat until frothy. Gradually add sugar and beat until soft peaks form. Pour mango slices in baked shell; top with meringue and bake at 325°F until mangoes are done. Meringue should be light brown in color.

MANGO CHIFFON PIE

Mango pulp can be used in guava chiffon pie recipe in place of guava pulp.

FRESH MANGO PIE

Yield: One 9-inch pie

2/3–3/4 c sugar
1-1/2–2 T enriched flour
1/8 t salt
1/2 t lemon rind, grated

1-1/2 t lemon juice
1/4 t nutmeg
1/2 t cinnamon
6 c half-ripe mangoes, sliced
pastry for 2-crust pie
1 T butter or margarine

Combine first seven ingredients. Place half of mangoes in pastry lined pie plate. Sprinkle half of sugar mixture over mangoes; add remaining mangoes and sprinkle with other half of sugar mixture. Dot with butter. Cover with remaining pastry and bake at 425°F for 40 to 50 minutes.

The amounts of sugar and flour in this recipe vary because mangoes differ widely in sweetness and in juiciness.

Mango Sherbet

Yield: 6 servings

3/4 c sugar
dash of salt
1 c water
1 c mango pulp
1/2 c heavy cream
1/4 c fresh lemon or orange juice
1/2 c mango chunks
2 egg whites

Combine 1/2 cup sugar, salt, and water; cook five minutes; then cool. Add mango to cooled syrup. Blend in lemon juice. Freeze in refrigerator tray until firm. Beat egg whites until frothy. Add remaining sugar, a tablespoon at a time, and continue beating until stiff peaks form. Turn frozen mixture into chilled bowl; break into chunks and beat until smooth. Fold in beaten egg whites and mango chunks. Return quickly to cold tray and freeze until firm. Spoon into sherbet dishes and garnish with mint.

Mango Chutney

16 c green or half-ripe mangoes, sliced
1/2 c Hawaiian salt
12 c sugar
3 c vinegar
2 c karo
2 c water
1 c ginger root, chopped fine
1 lb. raisins
6 medium onions, chopped in small pieces
2 T garlic, chopped fine
1 T ground cloves
1 T cinnamon
1 T ground nutmeg
1 c blanched almonds, cut in strips

12 small chili peppers, seeds removed
4 t salt, or to taste

Salt mangoes overnight in Hawaiian salt. When ready to make chutney, rinse. Boil syrup of sugar, vinegar, karo, water and ginger root for 15 minutes. Add mangoes by the handful to get them coated with syrup. Add remaining ingredients. Cook 1-1/2 to 2 hours or until chutney is thick and mangoes are tender (not mushy). Stir every 10 or 15 minutes to prevent burning. Pour into hot sterilized jars. Seal with paraffin.

Mountain Apples

These small apples grow wild in rainy valleys. The skin is a transparent coating of red or white color. The texture is similar to a Bartlett pear, only much more watery.

The flavor is very delicate, and other than sieving for juice, the best way to enjoy them is to eat them fresh. You might try freezing the pulp to be used in juices later.

Calories: 1 medium—15

Ohelo Berries

Found on a pretty little bush, ohelo berries are a tasty treat when picnicking or hiking. They have a smooth skin, are round and about the size of the tip of your little finger. When ripe, they are red, yellow, orange or gold. They grow only at high altitudes in Kula and Ukumehame Canyon on Maui and the volcano area on Hawai'i. Jelly made from this berry is especially pretty. The flavor should be enhanced with lemon or lime juice. Use a recipe from the pectin box or bottle for gooseberries.

Onions

❖Chopped onion may be frozen if it will be used in cooked dishes later.

Chopping Onions

Use blender when possible. It saves time and tears. Use wide rectangular Japanese chopping knife for dicing or Oriental slicing. Chop green onion quickly by cutting in three-inch lengths first, making a stack; then chopping all at once.

FRIED ONION RINGS

Yield: 8-10 servings

6 Kula onions, sliced 1/4" thick
2 c milk
3 eggs
all purpose flour

Separate onion slices into rings. Beat milk and eggs together thoroughly. Drop a few rings at a time into milk mixture. Shake off excess liquid, then drop into pan of flour. Fill frying basket one-fourth full to brown evenly. Set basket in deep, hot fat (375°F). Cook until crisp and golden. Stir once with fork to separate. Remove from fat. Drain on paper towel. Sprinkle with salt just before serving or rings lose their crispness.

ANN'S PICKLED ONIONS

3 qts. to 1 gal. onions, small, or halved medium
1/2 c Hawaiian salt
3 c sugar
3 c vinegar
1 T mustard seed (optional)
2 t celery seed (optional)
1/8 t cayenne pepper

Clean onions, salt and let stand overnight or longer. Drain; do not rinse. Combine vinegar, sugar and seasonings and bring to a boil. Add to onions. Pack while hot in clean jars. Let stand at least three days.

Panini

This cactus fruit is either red or white here. Because it is very difficult to get, it is considered a delicacy. Protective clothing is a necessity. Gloves in particular should be worn when cutting the fruit from the cactus. To open, hold fruit with a fork and slice off both ends. Slit skin with sharp knife along one side lengthwise. Roll the skin away from the fruit.

Squeeze panini for juice to add to other tropical juices, make the juice into jelly using powdered or liquid pectin, or slice the fruit for use as dessert or salad.

Papaya

❖ Slices soften less if frozen plain or with a sprinkling of dry sugar. Pulp freezes well.
Calories: One-half ripe—60.

GREEN PAPAYA PICKLE

1 green papaya
3/4 c water
1 small onion, sliced or chopped fine
1 t salt
1 t sugar
1 t vinegar

Peel papaya and remove seeds. Cut the papaya in quarters; grate fine. Put in saucepan and add water; boil for two minutes. Squeeze water out. Mix with onion, salt, sugar and vinegar and serve.

RIPE PAPAYA PICKLE

Yield: 4 cups

3 c sugar
1 c vinegar

2 t ginger, grated
1 t lemon juice
4 c firm and ripe papaya, diced

Boil sugar, vinegar and ginger until it threads, about 12 to 15 minutes. Add lemon juice. Drop in papaya and boil until it is transparent, about 30 minutes. Stir as little as possible so that pieces will not break.

Papaya Pie

1 c pineapple
3/4 c sugar
3 c papaya purée
1/3 c cornstarch
1/3 c water
1 T butter or margarine
pastry for 2-crust pie

Filling:

Heat juice and sugar to boiling. Add papaya and combine cornstarch and water. Cook until thickened, stirring constantly. Add butter.

Crust:

Prepare pastry for a double crust pie and line a 9-inch pie plate with half; pour in filling. Roll out remaining dough and cut strips 1/2-inch wide and about 11 inches long. Weave strips on waxed paper, slip hand underneath and quickly invert on pie. Trim lattice ends to edge of pan, seal with water and crimp with edge of lower crust. Bake at 425°F for 25 minutes.

Papaya Mold

Yield: 8 servings

1 3 oz. pkg. lime-flavored gelatin
1 3 oz. pkg. lemon-flavored gelatin
2 c hot water
1-1/2 c pineapple juice
4 c papaya cubes

Dissolve gelatin in hot water; add pineapple juice. Chill until partially set. Add papaya cubes. Pour into a 2-quart mold. Chill until firm. Unmold and fill center with Curried Tuna Salad. Garnish with pineapple slices.

Curried Tuna Salad

2 6-1/2 oz. cans tuna
1 c celery, diced
1/4 c green pepper, chopped
2 hard-cooked eggs, chopped
1 T onion, chopped
1/2 c mayonnaise
2 t lemon juice

1 t curry powder
1/2 t salt
1/4 t pepper

Combine tuna, celery, green pepper, eggs and onion. Blend remaining ingredients together; add to tuna mixture and toss lightly. Chill and serve in the center of molded fruit gelatin.

CHICKEN WITH PAPAYA (LAUYA)

1 whole stewing chicken
1 t salt
1 T patis (juice of salted fish) OR shoyu
2 medium-size green papayas, sliced 1/4" thick
small piece of ginger
7 c cold water

Cut up chicken, taking out excess fat. Clean and drain. In saucepan, cook chicken pieces with salt, patis and ginger for 20 minutes or until fat forms at the bottom of pan, stirring occasionally. Add water, cover and cook for about 2-1/2 hours or until tender. Add sliced papayas and cook for another 20 minutes.

PAPAYA CHIFFON PIE

Yield: One 9-inch pie

3 eggs, separated
1/2 c sugar
2 T lemon juice
1 t lemon rind, grated
3 T hot water
1/2 T unflavored gelatin
2 T cold water
1-3/4 c papaya pulp
1 baked pie shell

Beat egg yolks until thick; add 1/4 cup of the sugar, lemon juice and rind and hot water. Cook over low heat until mixture thickens. Soak gelatin in cold water and dissolve in the hot mixture. Add papaya pulp. Cool and fold in the egg whites which have been beaten with the remaining sugar. Pour into a baked pie shell and chill until firm.

PAPAYA AND SALTED NUT SALAD

Chill thoroughly one ripe papaya. Remove seeds, peel and cut into small cubes. Blend with thinly sliced salted peanuts and coarsely cut lettuce. Toss slightly with French dressing. Serve on lettuce leaves.

PAPAYA SEED DRESSING

1/2 c sugar
1 t seasoned salt

I t dry mustard
I c white vinegar or tarragon vinegar
2 c oil
I small onion, minced, or I t instant minced onion
2 T fresh papaya seeds

Place vinegar and dry ingredients in blender, turn on and gradually add oil and onion. Finally, add papaya seeds and blend only until they are cut to the size of coarse ground pepper. This piquant dressing is excellent for both fruit and green salads.

Passion Fruit (Lilikoi)

Passion fruit is an oval, thick-skinned yellow or purple fruit. It is the size of a very large plum. It is called "passion fruit" because the flower is a perfect Maltese cross symbolizing the Crucifixion.

Use passion fruit juices in place of lemon juice in your favorite lemon meringue pie.

Make juice by blending momentarily the seeds, then straining. A sieve may also be used.

❖ Passion fruit may be frozen satisfactorily as a juicy pulp or juice. Use one part sugar to five parts pulp. Package and freeze.

Calories: 1/2 cup unsweetened—53

PASSION FRUIT CHIFFON PIE (WITH FROZEN CONCENTRATE)

I-I/3 T gelatin
I/4 c water
3 T sugar
4 egg yolks
I/2 c passion fruit concentrate, undiluted
4 egg whites
6 T sugar
I 9" pie shell, baked

Soak gelatin in water. Beat sugar and egg yolks together. Cook in top of double boiler, stirring constantly, until thick. Remove from hot water. Add gelatin and stir until it dissolves. Cover and allow to cool for five minutes. While it is cooling, beat egg whites until they hold their shape. Beat in sugar 2 tablespoons at a time. Gradually stir passion fruit juice into the egg yolk mixture. As soon as mixture begins to set, fold in egg whites. Pour into pie shell and chill.

PASSION FRUIT-PEACH SOUFFLÉ SALAD

Yield: 6 servings

I T gelatin
I/3 c sweetened passion fruit juice
I/4 c sugar
I c hot water
2 T cold water

1/4 t salt
2 T lemon juice
1/2 c mayonnaise
1/2 c celery, diced
1 1 lb. can cling peach slices

Soften gelatin in passion fruit juice. Add sugar and hot water. Stir until thoroughly dissolved. Add water, salt, lemon juice and mayonnaise. Beat well with rotary beater. Pour into refrigerator freezing tray. Quick-chill in freezing unit 30 minutes, or until firm. Turn mixture into bowl and whip with rotary beater until fluffy. Fold in celery and 1-1/2 cups diced cling peaches. Pour into 1-quart mold or individual molds. Chill until firm in refrigerator, 60 minutes or more. Unmold and garnish with salad greens and remaining peaches.

LILIKOI MUFFINS

2 c sifted flour
1/2 c sugar
3 t baking powder
1/2 t salt
1/4 c margarine, melted
1 egg
1/2 c sweetened lilikoi juice
1/2 c milk

Sift flour, sugar, baking powder and salt. Then add margarine, egg, lilikoi juice and milk; mix. Fill 12 greased muffin cups two-thirds full of batter. Bake at 400°F for 20 minutes.

PASSION FRUIT SHERBET

Yield: 6 servings

1 c passion fruit juice
1/2 c sugar
1/2 c water
1/4 c lemon juice
1/2 c sugar
1/3 c water
1/4 t salt
2 egg whites

Combine the first four ingredients and stir until the sugar is dissolved. Pour into freezing tray of electric refrigerator and freeze to a mush. Meanwhile boil 1/2 cup sugar and 1/3 cup water until it spins a thread two inches long. Cool slightly. Beat egg whites and salt until stiff and your syrup slowly over them, beating constantly. Fold into the fruit mixture and continue to freeze. Stir once during freezing.

FRESH PASSION FRUIT CHIFFON PIE

Yield: One 9-inch pie

4 eggs, separated

1 c sugar
1/2 t salt
1/2 c lilikoi juice
1 T unflavored gelatin
1/4 c cold water
1 t lemon rind, grated
1 pie shell, baked
1/2 c cream, whipped

Beat egg yolks until thick. Add 1/2 cup of the sugar, salt, and lilikoi juice. Cook over low heat until thick, stirring constantly. Add gelatin which has been softened in the cold water, stirring until gelatin is dissolved. Add lemon rind and cool until slightly congealed. Fold in stiffly beaten egg whites to which the remaining 1/2 cup sugar has been added. Pour into baked pie shell and chill until firm. Serve with whipped cream.

CRYSTAL PASSION FRUIT PIE

Gelatin:
1 T unflavored gelatin
1/4 c water
1 c boiling water
1/4 c sugar
1/2 c passion fruit juice

Pudding:
1/2 c sugar
1/4 c cornstarch
1/4 t salt
1 c milk
1/2 c passion fruit juice
2 eggs
1 T butter or margarine

Soften gelatin in 1/4 cup water; dissolve in boiling water. Add sugar, stir until dissolved; add juice. Pour into flat pan and chill until set. Cut into small squares and fold into cooled pudding.

Combine sugar cornstarch and salt in heavy pan. Blend in milk, passion fruit juice, eggs and butter. Cook until thick and smooth, stirring constantly. Cool. Fold gelatin into pudding and pour into No-Roll Coconut Crust. Chill.

SWEET 'N TART PASSION PIE

Yield: One 8-inch or 9-inch pie

1 pt. (1/2 qt.) vanilla ice cream
3 eggs
1/4 c sugar
1/4 t salt
1/4 c frozen passion fruit concentrate
1 c whipping cream

Cut ice cream in 1/2-inch slices; lay on bottom of pan to cover. Cut remaining slices in half; arrange around pan to make rim. Fill spots with ice cream where needed. With tip of spoon, smooth "crust." Freeze until firm before adding filling.

Beat together one whole egg and two yolks. Add sugar, salt and passion fruit concentrate. Cook over low heat, stirring constantly until thick. Cool. Beat egg whites until stiff; then whip cream (no need to wash beaters). Fold cream into passion fruit mixture. Next, fold in egg whites. Pour into ice cream shell. Freeze.

PASSION FRUIT JELLY WITH POWDERED PECTIN

Yield: About five 6-oz. glasses

1/2 c passion fruit juice (3 lb. passion fruit)
3-1/2 c or 1-1/2 lb. sugar
2 c water
1 box (2-1/2 oz.) powdered pectin

Measure sugar and 1 cup water into a saucepan. Mix well. Heat to dissolve sugar, stirring constantly. Remove from heat and add passion fruit juice. Set aside. Mix powdered pectin and remaining 1 cup water in small saucepan. Bring to boil, boil hard for one minute, stirring. Pour hot dissolved pectin into passion fruit-sugar mixture and stir for two minutes. Pour jelly into hot containers and seal.

PASSION FRUIT JELLY WITH LIQUID PECTIN

Yield: About four 6-oz. glasses

1/2 c passion fruit juice (3 lb. passion fruit)
3 c sugar
1 c water
1/2 bottle liquid pectin

Mix sugar and water together in a kettle. Boil for one minute vigorously, stirring. Remove from heat. Stir in liquid pectin. Add passion fruit juice and mix well. Skim off foam. Pour jelly into hot containers and seal.

Peaches—Green

PEACH UME

1 gal. green peaches
1 c Hawaiian salt
6 c vinegar
6 c sugar
1/2 bottle red food coloring

Wash and soak peaches in water to cover and 1 cup salt for 1-1/2 days. Dry for one day. Boil remaining ingredients and cool. Put dried peaches in gallon jar and pour syrup over them. Let stand at least one week.

Pepeiau

Pepeiau means ear in Hawaiian. It is a fungus that grows on logs in damp areas. It is dried for later use rather than frozen. Simply place pepeiau in a shallow box and place outside in the shade. When dry, store in cool, dry area.

To use, soak in salted water until softened. Salt removes any dirt that may have settled on the fungus. Usually 1/2 hour is enough soaking. Use in sukiyaki, chop suey, soups or other shoyu dishes.

Peppers

Many varieties of peppers grow in Hawaii. All but the bell peppers are very hot. Use sparingly in cooking. Do not touch seeds with bare hands. Use rubber gloves.

PICKLED PEPPERS

6 large hot peppers
5 large bell peppers

Seed hot peppers, being careful to use gloves and old knife. In an old container cook the hot peppers until soft outside or in well-ventilated room. Clean bell peppers; cut them in quarters. Cook until soft in separate container, covered with water. When cooked and cooled, place peppers in quart-size jar—hot peppers on the bottom and the sweet peppers on top. Pour white vinegar to completely cover peppers. Add 1 tablespoon Hawaiian salt. Cover jar and shake a few times to evenly distribute the salt. Let stand a week in refrigerator before using.

PORTUGUESE PICKLED TURKEY

Rub turkey well with Portuguese Pickling. Marinate in pickling liquid for at least 24 hours. Roast in 300°F oven.

Pickling:
I medium clove garlic
I large piece pickled pepper
1/2 t Portuguese spice
salt to taste (about I T)
I T vinegar
1-1/4 c water

Mash garlic and pepper. Add spice and salt, a tablespoon to start with. Add vinegar and water. Stir well until salt is dissolved.

PORTUGUESE SPICE

2 bottles whole anise
I bottle stick cinnamon
I bottle whole cloves
I bottle whole peppercorns

Put all spices in large flat pan and toast in 300°F oven until crisp—about 30 minutes. Grind in blender or spice grinder until fine. Store in the bottles. Because this makes a lot of spice, find four or five persons to share the spices and the cost.

Portuguese Poultry Stuffing

Cook gizzards, liver and neck of turkey in enough water to cover. Simmer until well done. Extra gizzards may be added. When cooked, save the broth.

1 8 oz. Portuguese sausage
1 loaf (1 lb.) dry bread
1/4 c round onion, finely minced
1/4 c green onion, finely minced
1/8 c parsley, finely chopped
1 c cottage roll ham, chopped
5 medium eggs
1 piece pickled pepper (for hot dressing add
   large piece; for mild, a smaller portion)
1/2 t Portuguese spice
salt to taste

Chop all meats. Soak bread in enough of the broth to soften well. Add softened bread and meats to all other ingredients and mix well. Place in baking pan and cover well with foil. Bake in 300°F preheated oven for one hour and 15 minutes or until done. Baste with turkey drippings about three times during cooking period.

Roast Potatoes

Peel desired amount of Irish potatoes. Add a little more water and salt to the left-over pickling used for the turkey roast. Soak potatoes in liquid for one-half hour. Remove from liquid and place them in a pan with fat from roasted turkey (beef or pork). Roast in 375°F oven in an open pan. Turn potatoes often to brown well on all sides. When half-done, taste for salt and add if necessary.

Persimmons

Customarily served raw, spooned out of the skin. Lemon or lime juice enhances flavor. Use sliced in salads; pulp in ice cream, milk drinks, pudding sauces, pies and cookies.

❖ Pulp freezes well. When ripe, persimmons are bright red-orange and look soft. Avoid cooking because the flavor becomes astringent. Stir into cooked and cooled puddings or pie fillings.
Calories: One fruit—103

Persimmon Pudding

1 c persimmon pulp (fruit should be fully ripe)
1 c sweet whole milk
1 t butter, melted
pinch of salt
1/4 t cinnamon
2 t soda
1 c all-purpose flour, sifted
1 t vanilla

Mix the ingredients in the order given and beat well. Place in the well-buttered top of a double boiler and steam for two hours, or until a toothpick inserted comes out dry. Serve hot or cold with one of the following sauces:

Whipped Cream Sauce
I egg
I/2 c sugar
I/2 c whipped cream
I T brandy

Beat the egg well with sugar. Fold in whipped cream. Add brandy.

Hard Sauce:
I t cornstarch
dash of salt
2 T sugar
I t butter
water
3/4 c boiling water
I t whiskey or rum

Cream together cornstarch, salt, sugar and butter. Add a few drops of water to soften. Add boiling water and boil over moderate heat for four to five minutes stirring constantly. Add whiskey or rum before serving.

PERSIMMON CAKE

Yield: Two loaves

2 c nuts, chopped
2 c raisins
2 c persimmon, mashed
2 c white sugar
2 T corn oil
3 c flour
I/4 t cloves
2 t cinnamon
2 t soda
I t salt
I c milk
I t vanilla

Mix nuts, raisins, persimmon pulp, sugar and oil. Sift flour, spices, soda and salt and add to above mixture alternately with milk and vanilla. Pour into well-oiled loaf pans and bake at 325°F for 1-1/4 hours or until done.

PERSIMMON COOKIES

Yield: 4 dozen

I/2 c margarine
I c sugar
I egg
I c persimmon pulp
I t salt

1 c raisins
1 c nuts, chopped
3 c flour
1 t cinnamon
1/2 t nutmeg
1/2 t salt
1 t vanilla

Cream margarine and sugar until fluffy; add egg and beat well. Add persimmon pulp and soda; mix well. Fold in remaining ingredients that have been mixed together. Drop on oiled cookie sheet. Bake at 350°F for 10 to 12 minutes.

Pineapple

❖ Pack with one part sugar to six to eight parts of pineapple depending on sweetness of fruit. Small cubes of pineapple added to papaya and then frozen make a nice combination.

Hint: Do not use fresh pineapple in gelatin without first boiling it for a few minutes. Raw pineapple has an enzyme that digests the gelatin which prevents setting.

Calories: One wedge—60; 1 cup cubes—68

FRESH PINEAPPLE PIE

2 eggs
1-1/2 c sugar
1 T lemon juice
2 c pineapple, shredded
pastry for double crust pie
2 T butter

Beat eggs, add sugar, lemon juice and pineapple. Pour into pie plate lined with crust. Dot with butter; cover with pastry and sprinkle sugar and cinnamon on top. Bake 10 minutes at 450°F; 35 minutes at 350°F.

PINEAPPLE WHIPPED CREAM PIE

Yield: One 9-inch pie

1 pkg. coconut or butterscotch nut cookie dough
2 T cornstarch
2 T sugar
1/4 t salt
1/4 c water
2 c fresh pineapple, chopped, or 1 20-oz. can crushed pineapple, drained
1 c whipping cream

Slice cookie dough in 1/4-inch slices. Arrange slices in 9-inch pie pan, first lining bottom of pan, then sides. (Let side slices rest on bottom layer to make higher sides.) Bake in 375°F oven until lightly browned, 9 to 12 minutes. Cool, Combine remaining ingredients, except cream, in saucepan. Cook and stir over medium heat until thickened. Cool. Fold into whipped cream. Pour into cooled crust. Chill or serve immediately.

PINEAPPLE CHUTNEY

Yield: 4 pints

I medium pineapple, 4 c chopped
I-1/2 c vinegar
I-1/2 c brown sugar
I 15 oz. pkg. raisins
I T salt
2 T ginger root, finely chopped
2 T garlic (5 cloves), finely chopped
3 Hawaiian red peppers, seeded and finely chopped
I c almonds or macadamia nuts, chopped

Peel and core pineapple; cut into small pieces. Combine with all other ingredients except nuts. Cook slowly until pineapple is tender, about one-half hour. Add nuts and cook until chutney is of desired consistency. Stir frequently to prevent scorching. Pour into sterilized jars and seal or cover with paraffin.

SUSAN'S PINEAPPLE MUFFINS

Yield: 12 muffins

2 c flour
3 t baking powder
I t salt
1/4 t soda
1/3 c sugar
I egg
4 t butter
1/2 c milk
1/2 c pineapple juice drained from crushed pineapple
3/4 c crushed pineapple, drained
1/3 c pineapple, crushed
1/3 c macadamia nuts, chopped

Sift flour, measure, then sift all dry ingredients together. Mix together egg, melted butter, milk, pineapple juice and 3/4 cup crushed pineapple. Add liquids to a well in center of dry ingredients. Mix only until combined, mixture will be lumpy. Fill pans to approximately one-third full. Mix 1/3 cup pineapple and macadamia nuts together and spread on top of unbaked muffins. Bake at 400°F for 20 to 23 minutes.

PINEAPPLE JAM

Yield: Nine 6-oz. glasses

3 c pineapple pulp, drained (I large pineapple)
3/4 c pineapple juice
1/4 c lemon juice

7 c sugar
1 bottle liquid pectin

Drain pineapple; measure pulp into large saucepan, add juices and sugar; mix well. Place over high heat, bring to a full rolling boil and boil hard for one minute, stirring constantly. Remove from heat and stir in liquid pectin. Stir and skim for five minutes to prevent floating fruit. Ladle into hot sterilized glasses and cover with paraffin at once.

Plum

. . . .

❖ To freeze, pack in either dry sugar or in syrup. Packing in dry sugar gives a better flavor, but skins are somewhat tougher. Plum purée is an excellent frozen product. Use one part sugar to three to five parts of fruit. Pack and freeze.
Calories: One fruit—22

To Can Plums

Use plums that are ripe (for best flavor), but still firm.

Wash, remove stems and any defective parts. Prick skin generously with a big needle. Put whole plums into a kettle of boiling #2 syrup (2 cups of water to 1 cup sugar) for about 15 seconds, to slightly shrink the fruit and insure a firm pack. Remove from syrup and pack into clean jars. (A better pack can be had if, after the boiling syrup treatment, the plums are cut into halves.)

Pack the fruit to within one-half inch of the top of the jars, then add enough of the boiling syrup to completely fill the jars.

Place the open jars in a large vessel of boiling water on a rack or cloth and cover the vessel loosely. Allow the water bath to come back to a boil then count the time. Boil for 10 minutes.

Then lift the jars from the water long enough to add more syrup if necessary, wipe off rim of jars, put on caps and rings, "snugly" only, and return the jars immediately to the hot water. Add enough boiling water to completely submerge jars.

Start timing when water returns to a boil. Boil (this is called "processing") for full 15 minutes.

Then remove the jars from the water and allow to cool, the rings may be removed for using again. Label and store the canned plums.

PLUM JELLY

Yield: 10 medium glasses

3-1/2 c plum juice (about 4 lb. ripe plums)
1/4 c lemon juice, strained
6-1/2 c sugar
1/2 bottle Certo fruit pectin

Crush about 4 pounds fully ripe plums. Do not peel or pit. Add 1 cup water, bring to boil and simmer, covered, 10 minutes. Place in jelly cloth or bag and let juice drip.

Measure 3-1/2 cups plum juice and 1/4 cup lemon juice into large saucepan.

Add sugar and mix well. Place over high heat and bring to boil, stirring constantly. At once stir in Certo. Then bring to a full rolling boil and boil hard one minute, stirring constantly. Remove from heat, skim off excess foam with metal spoon and pour into hot, sterilized jars or glasses. Cover at once with 1/8-inch hot paraffin.

PLUM COBBLER

Yield: 6 servings

2 c red plums, sliced and pitted
1 c sugar
2 T cornstarch
1 c water
1 T butter
1/2 t cinnamon
2 c prepared biscuit mix
2 T sugar
2/3 c milk

Preheat oven to hot (400°F). Combine plums, sugar and cornstarch in saucepan. Add water and cook, stirring constantly, until mixture comes to a boil. Remove from heat and stir in butter and cinnamon. Pour into greased 1-1/2 quart casserole. Place in hot oven while you prepare biscuit topping.

Combine biscuit mix and sugar. Add milk and stir to make a soft dough with fork: beat 20 strokes. Drop by spoonful on top of hot plum mixture. Place in hot oven (400°F) and bake 25 minutes or until biscuit topping is brown and juice is bubbly. Serve warm in bowls, topped with juices from cobbler and ice cream, or pass a bowl of whipped cream.

PLUM COFFEE CAKE

Filling:
1–1-1/2 c plums, sliced
1/2 c brown sugar
1 t cinnamon
1/2 c nuts, chopped, or raisins
1 T butter
1 T flour

Batter (may use cake mix):
1/2 c butter
1 c sugar
2 eggs, separated
1-1/2 c flour
1 t salt
2 t baking powder
1 T each grated lemon and orange peel (optional)
1/2 c milk

Cream butter and sugar, add yolks and mix. Stir in sifted dry ingredients. Add orange and lemon peel and milk. Fold in stiffly beaten egg whites. Grease a 9-inch pan. Put in three-fourths of the batter. Add sliced, peeled fresh or frozen plums and filling. Pour remaining batter over filling. Bake at 350°F for 40 to 45 minutes.

Plums—Wild Hawaiian

Small, dark purple plums grow on large trees in wetter areas such as Iao Valley and Waihee. They are too ripe for eating after they have fallen from the tree, but children climb the trees and pick these very astringent fruits.

Poha

This is called "Lantern Fruit" on the mainland because the cage enclosing the edible fruit is pretty enough to be a coachman's lantern.

❖ These fruits may be frozen as is, or crushed and frozen as pulp.

Calories: 2/3 cup—48

POHA JAM

Yield: Five 6-oz. glasses

3 c raw poha (about 3 lb.)
I c sugar per each cup cooked poha
1/4 c water
I T lemon juice (optional)

Sort, husk and wash poha. Place whole fruit and 1/4 cup water in a kettle. Cook slowly for 30 minutes. Stir frequently until there is sufficient liquid to prevent fruit from scorching. Let fruit stand for five to six hours.

Measure poha pulp and juice and add an equal quantity of sugar. Cook slowly, about one hour. Add lemon juice and stir frequently until juice thickens slightly or gives a jam test. Ladle into hot containers and seal immediately.

DOUBLE CRUST POHA PIE

Yield: One 9-inch pie

pastry for 2-crust pie
4 c poha
I c sugar
2 T cornstarch
1/4 t nutmeg
I T lemon juice
I T butter or margarine

Line 9-inch pie plate with pastry. Cut each poha in half. Put half of the poha in pie shell and sprinkle with half of the combined sugar, cornstarch, and nutmeg. Repeat, using remainder of poha and sugar mixture. Sprinkle with lemon juice; dot with butter. Cover with crust and bake at 450°F for 10 minutes. Reduce heat to 350°F and bake 40 minutes longer.

Pomelo
· · · · · · ·

This fruit could be called the Hawaiian grapefruit. It is about twice the size of a grapefruit, but most of the size is lost when the very thick citrus-like skin is peeled away. Inside, it is like a coarse grapefruit texture. Hundreds of seeds cluster at the center of each section. Flavor is much like grapefruit, but leaves a bitter taste in the mouth that some find objectionable. It can be used as a juice or fruit in salad. The juice combines well with tangerine in making tangerine jelly.

❖ Freeze the juice with 1 tablespoon sugar to each cup to preserve the flavor.

Potatoes
· · · · · · ·

Cooked potatoes may be frozen if they will later be steamed or used in cooked dishes. If used directly from the freezer, they are grainy in texture.

POTATO PANCAKES

8 large potatoes
3 island eggs
I onion
salt and pepper to taste

Peel and wash, then dry the potatoes and grate them. They will be quite watery. Drain them well and add beaten egg yolks, then the stiffly beaten egg whites. Add onion, chopped fine, and seasonings. Fry in shortening or butter until brown. Serve with bacon and applesauce.

PORTUGUESE RED BEAN SOUP

3 ham shanks
I linguesa
I small soup bone
2 c dried red beans, soaked overnight
I can tomato sauce
1/4 t Portuguese spice
2 T oil
I medium-size round onion, sliced
3 T parsley, minced
2 large potatoes, diced

Boil ham shanks, linguesa and soup bone in enough water to cover. When meat is almost done, add beans and cook until done. Add tomato sauce and spice. In oil, fry onion slices and parsley until tender. Add to soup stock. Add potatoes and cook until done. Salt to taste. Other vegetables, such as cabbage, watercress, carrots, etc. may be added to this soup.

PORTUGUESE WHITE BREAD

Yield: 4 loaves

I medium potato, peeled and grated
1/2 t sugar

1-1/2 c warm water
2 pkg. dry yeast
10 c regular flour, sifted
1 c sugar
1-1/4 t salt
1 T shortening

Combine grated potato, sugar, water and yeast in small bowl. Cover with plate and let it begin to rise. In large pan or bowl, combine flour, sugar and salt. Pour in yeast mixture and mix until smooth. Have a bowl of warm water near and add a little occasionally while kneading with fist. Knead until large bubbles begin to show in dough, about one-half hour. Add shortening and knead a few more times, then rub shortening on the outside of dough. Cover with clean cloth, then wrap pan and cloth with large blanket or sheet. Place in oven that has been slightly warmed. Let rise until triple in bulk. Make into buns or loaves. Let rise again until double in bulk, then bake at 350°F for 45 minutes for loaves or 20 minutes for buns.

CHOCOLATE POTATO CAKE

1 c cooked potato, grated
1-1/2 c flour
1/2 t cinnamon
2 t baking powder
1/2 t salt
1 c nuts, chopped
2 c sugar
1 c butter
4 eggs
1 c chocolate, grated (4 squares)
1/2 c milk

Cream butter, add sifted sugar and cream well. Separate eggs and add yolks one at a time. Stir in chocolate and nuts, then chilled grated potato. Add sifted dry ingredients alternately with milk. Fold in egg whites, beaten with 1/8 teaspoon salt. Bake at 350°F in large sheet cake pan, one hour. Frost as desired. Delicious and moist as is.

BONNIE'S POTATO SALAD

5 Irish potatoes
5 eggs, hard cooked
1-1/2 t salt
1/2 t pepper
1 large onion, chopped
2 T pickle relish
1-1/2 c mayonnaise
1/2 c grated raw carrot
1/2 c cooked peas

Scrub potatoes and boil (unpeeled) in water until tender. Cool, peel and dice in 1/2-inch cubes. Dice eggs. Add salt, pepper, onion, pickle relish. Mix well. Add mayonnaise, carrot and peas. Toss until well mixed. Chill overnight.

Pumpkin
. . . .

❖ Cook until tender, mash, package and freeze. Cubes may be frozen if they are blanched in boiling salted water for three to four minutes, plunged in ice water for the same length of time and packaged.

Fresh Pumpkin Pie

I 9" pie shell, unbaked
I c granulated sugar
1/2 t salt
1-1/2 t cinnamon
1/2 t nutmeg
1/2 t ginger
1/2 t cloves
1/2 t allspice
1-1/2 c fresh, cooked pumpkin*
1-2/3 c (I large can) evaporated milk, undiluted
2 eggs

Mix filling ingredients until smooth. Place in unbaked pie shell. Bake in hot oven (425°F) for 15 minutes. Lower temperature to moderate (350°F) and continue baking for about 35 minutes or until custard is firm.

*Peel and seed pumpkin. Cut into one-inch cubes. Cook in small amount of salty water until tender. Mash as for mashed potatoes and use in pumpkin pie.

Pumpkin may be baked in oven, then mashed.

Pumpkin Cake

2-1/4 c flour
3 t baking powder
1/2 t salt
1/4 t soda
1-1/2 t cinnamon
1/2 t ginger
1/2 t allspice
1/4 c butter
I c brown sugar
1/2 c sugar
I egg plus 2 egg yolks, unbeaten
3/4 c sour milk
3/4 c canned pumpkin
1/2 c walnuts, finely chopped

Measure sifted flour, add baking powder, salt, soda and spices. Sift together three times. Cream butter, add sugar gradually and cream well. Add egg and egg yolks, one at a time, beating until light. Add flour alternately with sour milk, in small amounts, beating after each addition until smooth. Add pumpkin and nuts; mix well. Bake 40 minutes at 350°F in 9x13-inch pan.

Pumpkin Muffins

Yield: 16 medium-size muffins

I c flour, sifted

1/2 c sugar

2 t baking powder

1/2 t cinnamon

1/2 t nutmeg

1/4 t salt

1/4 c butter

I egg, beaten

1/2 c canned pumpkin

1/2 c evaporated milk

1/2 c seedless raisins (optional)

I T sugar

Sift together in mixing bowl the flour, 1/2 cup sugar, baking powder, cinnamon, nutmeg and salt. Cut in butter until mixture resembles cornmeal. Combine beaten egg with canned pumpkin and evaporated milk. Stir in raisins. Add egg mixture to dry ingredients, stirring just enough to mix lightly. Fill greased muffin pans two-thirds full. Sprinkle 1/4 teaspoon sugar over each muffin. Bake in preheated oven (400°F) for 20 to 25 minutes until muffins are nicely browned.

Pumpkin Tea Loaf

Yield: One loaf

2 c all-purpose flour, sifted

1/2 t baking soda

1-1/2 t baking powder

3/4 t salt

I t cinnamon

1/2 t nutmeg

1/4 t ginger

1/2 c molasses

I c canned or cooked pumpkin, strained

1/2 c shortening

I t vanilla extract

1/4 t orange rind, grated

3/4 c sugar

2 eggs

I c chopped walnuts

Sift together first seven ingredients. Combine pumpkin and molasses. Cream together shortening, vanilla, orange rind and sugar until well blended. Add eggs, one at a time; beat after each addition. Add dry ingredients and liquid ingredients alternately, a little of each at a time; stir well after each addition. Stir in walnuts. Turn into greased and floured 9-1/2x5-1/4x2-3/4-inch loaf pan. Bake in a 350°F oven 55 to 65 minutes. Cool 10 minutes before removing from pan. When cold, frost with following frosting.

Cream together 3 tablespoons butter, 1 cup sifted confectioner's sugar and 1/4 teaspoon vanilla extract; add about 1 tablespoon strained, fresh orange juice; blend to spreading consistency.

Rhubarb

RHUBARB JAM

Yield: 8 medium glasses

3 c prepared fruit (about 1-1/2 lb.)
5-1/2 c sugar
1/2 bottle fruit pectin

Slice unpeeled rhubarb in 1/2-inch pieces. Simmer with 3/4 cup water, covered, until soft (about one minute).

Measure 3 cups soft fruit into a very large saucepan. Add sugar and mix well. Place over high heat, bring to a full rolling boil, and boil hard one minute, stirring constantly. Remove from heat and at once stir in Certo. Skim off foam with metal spoon. Then stir and skim for five minutes to cool slightly and to prevent floating fruit. Ladle into hot, sterilized glasses. Cover at once with 1/8-inch hot paraffin.

RHUBARB PIE

1 lb. rhubarb
2 c sugar
2 T flour
2 t cinnamon
1 egg
2 T butter

Wash and cut rhubarb but do not skin. Stir sugar, flour and cinnamon together. Add beaten egg and melted butter. Mix all together in a bowl. Line deep pie plate with pastry. Add filling and cover with top crust. Bake 45 minutes in hot over (400°F).

STEWED RHUBARB

Wash rhubarb, remove leaves. Cut in 1/2-inch pieces. Add water almost to cover and sugar, to taste. Cook until very soft, about 15 minutes. Serve on ice cream or with milk as a pudding.

❖ This dish may be frozen.

RHUBARB ANGEL FOOD CAKE

1 10" angel food or lemon chiffon cake
1 lb. fresh rhubarb
1/4 c sugar
2 T water
few drops of red food coloring
2 c whipping cream
2 T confectioner's sugar

Remove a 1/2-inch layer from top of cake. Hollow out inside of the cake to form a shell 1/2-inch thick on sides and bottom. Save the crumbs. Cook rhubarb with 1/4 cup sugar and water (or use 1-1/2 cups sweetened rhubarb sauce). Add food coloring to rhubarb and cool. Whip 1 cup whipping cream and fold in rhubarb and 1 cup cake crumbs. Fill cake shell with mixture and replace top layer. Frost cake with remaining cup of cream whipped and sweetened with 2 tablespoons confectioner's sugar.

Rice and Long Rice

❖ Rice can be frozen if it is steamed, reheated, or added to a casserole later. Otherwise, rice will be grainy in texture.

Quick-cooking rice is rarely used in Hawaii because the regular rice is superior in flavor and texture. In pan or rice pot, wash rice six or seven times in cold water. Drain and add the same amount of water as rice. Place over high heat until rice comes to a full boil. Turn heat to low, cover and cook 20 to 25 minutes. When steam stops rising from under the lid, rice is done.

RICE FOR SUSHI

3 c rice, washed
3-1/2 c water

Place on high heat until rice boils. Boil rapidly about five minutes, then simmer about 30 minutes. Turn heat off, but leave pot on element for another 10 minutes. Put rice in large container to cool. Toss to help cool slightly.

VINEGAR FOR SUSHI RICE

1 c Japanese vinegar
few dried shrimps, chopped, or 2 T shrimp, shredded
3/4 c sugar
2 T salt
1 t MSG
1 t ginger, chopped

Soak shrimp in vinegar for one hour. Remove shrimp from vinegar by straining. Add sugar, salt, MSG and chopped ginger to vinegar. Stir until dissolved, then toss with warm rice.

MOLDED SUSHI

Press the warm, prepared rice firmly into wooden molds. Push sushi out and garnish with red ebi (shrimp) flakes, fried egg wedges and a parsley leaf. Small round sushi may be dipped into red or green shrimp flakes.

KAMABOKO SUSHI

Cut pink-edged fish cake from board. Slice away the end pieces, then make slit 1/4-inch wide and almost through. Cut again 1/2-inch wide and all the way through.

Open kamaboko and stuff with prepared rice. Place 3/8-inch wide strip of nori across rice to look like a ribbon holding the kamaboko together.

SPANISH RICE

2-1/2 c pigeon peas
2 T red oil made with ahchote seed
1 lb. pork or Portuguese sausage
3 or 4 cloves garlic, mashed
1 medium onion, chopped
1 8 oz. can tomato sauce
salt
black pepper
2 c raw rice

Boil peas in water to cover about 10 minutes. Pour off water, cover with fresh water and boil again about 15 minutes. Make red oil by heating cooking oil or Crisco with ahchote (seeds from the lipstick plant). Fry pork in red oil until lightly browned. Add onion, garlic, and fry a few minutes. Add tomato sauce, salt and black pepper. Add the boiled beans and cook for 25 minutes. Add rice and cook until rice is tender. Garnish with thin slices of Portuguese sausage.

HAMBURGER AND LONG RICE

Yield: 4 servings

2 T oil
1 t rock salt
1 clove garlic, mashed
1 lb. hamburger
1 lb. string beans, cut diagonally
1 medium onion, sliced
2 c water
1 bunch long rice, soaked, drained and cut in 2" pieces
3 T shoyu
1/4 t MSG (optional)

Heat large pot or skillet; add oil, then stir-fry salt and garlic. Remove garlic. Add hamburger and brown well. Stir in beans, onion, water and soaked long rice. Simmer until beans are just tender, about two minutes. Stir in shoyu and MSG.

CHICKEN AND LONG RICE

2-1/2 to 3 lb. stewing chicken, cut in pieces
2 T oil
1 clove garlic
1" piece ginger
4 c water
1 bundle long rice, soaked in cold water 1/2 hour
1 T salt
dash of pepper

1 T shoyu
1 t MSG

Garnish:
2 eggs
2 stalks green onion

Fry garlic and ginger in 2 tablespoons oil (chicken fat may be used) until brown. Remove garlic and ginger. Fry chicken until slightly browned. Add water and cook until chicken is tender (about 2 to 2-1/2 hours). Add long rice and seasonings. Cook 10 minutes longer. Garnish: Beat eggs lightly, add chopped green onions. Season with salt and pepper. Fry into thin sheets. Cut in 1/2-inch squares and add to chicken and long rice.

BEEF WITH LONG RICE

Yield: 4 servings

1 lb. beef
1/2 bundle long rice
oil for deep frying
2 medium onions, sliced thin
1/2 head lettuce, shredded

Marinade:
2 T flour
2 t sugar
1 T shoyu
2 T wine
1-1/2 t ginger root, minced

Gravy:
2 t cornstarch
1 T shoyu
3/4 c water
1/2 t salt
1/4 t MSG
1" piece ginger

Garnish:
1 bunch green onion, chopped fine

Slice beef thin, soaking marinade 1/2 hour.

Using scissors, cut dry long rice into three-inch lengths. Deep fry a small handful of long rice at a time; it puffs instantly. Drain on absorbent paper. Line large platter with shredded lettuce. Place drained long rice on lettuce. Stir-fry onion in 1 tablespoon oil for two minutes, arrange on puffed long rice. Stir-fry meat in 1 tablespoon oil for two minutes, arrange on onion. Mix gravy ingredients together. Bring to a boil. When slightly thickened, pour over meat. Garnish with green onion.

Rose Apple

When ripe, this fruit is yellow with rose tints to its outer skin. It is quite hollow inside with one seed in this hollow area. Eat skin and delicately flavored fruit.

Roselle

ROSELLE JELLY

Yield: About four 6-oz. glasses

3 croselle juice (2 lb. whole roselles and 6 c water)
2-1/4 c sugar

Wash fruit thoroughly; do not remove calyxes from seeds. Add water. Place kettle over heat, cover, bring to a boil quickly and cook until calyxes are soft (about seven minutes). Extract juice by straining.

Measure juice into a shallow kettle. Add sugar and stir well. Boil over high heat to 8°F above boiling point of water, or until jelly mixture sheets from a spoon. Remove from heat; skim off foam quickly. Pour jelly immediately into hot containers and seal.

Sweet and Sour Sop (Cherimoya)

Sweet sop is the Island name for Cherimoya. It is shaped like an elongated apple with a beautifully designed skin. Scalloped would be an appropriate word for the rough-looking exterior. It feels velvet soft between the ridges made by the design. It is green and firm when ready to be picked; brownish-green and soft when ready to eat. Black seeds are spaced throughout the flesh. Serve chilled, split in half, and flavored with lemon or orange juice. Eat with a spoon.

❖ Freeze as a purée. Scoop out flesh and press through sieve to remove seeds. Add 1 tablespoon lemon juice and 2 tablespoons sugar to each cup to preserve the flavor and color.

Use in salad dressings, dessert toppings or blended in fruit juices. Flavor blends well with that of bananas and pineapple.

Sour sop is similar to sweet sop in texture and appearance. It is larger in size and decidedly sour.

❖Freeze as a purée and add one part sugar to six parts fruit. Excellent in beverages, sherbets and ice creams.

Custard apple comes with either rough or smooth skin. The texture inside is much like the sweet or sour sop, but very sweet in taste.

Jack fruit is another similar fruit, but this one is easily recognized. It grows from either trunks or branches of trees and is extremely large in size. It reaches the size of a basketball or more.

Calories: 1/2 cup purée—64

Sweet Sop Ice Cream

Yield: Makes 1-1/4 quarts

1/2 c sugar
1-1/2 t cornstarch
2 T orange juice
1 T vanilla
dash of salt
2 egg yolks
2 c heavy cream
3 c sweet sop purée

Combine all ingredients in blender or mixer bowl. Blend or beat until smooth. Freeze until almost firm in 1-1/2-quart container. Beat until smooth. Return to freezer until firm.

Sour Sop Ade

3-1/2 c sour sop juice
2-2/3 c water
1 c sugar
2-2/3 T lemon juice

Mix ingredients until sugar is dissolved. Pour over cracked ice.

Sour Sop Sherbet

1 c sugar
2 c water
2 c sour sop purée
1 T lemon juice
1 egg white

Boil sugar and water for five minutes. Cool to lukewarm. Add remaining ingredients. Freeze in ice cream freezer using eight parts ice to one part salt. This may be frozen in trays if beaten twice during the freezing process—once when mushy and once when almost frozen solid.

Soybeans

❖ Green pods may be blanched in boiling water for two minutes, plunged into ice water for two minutes and frozen in plastic bags. Use in recipes below or as substitute for lima or cooked navy beans.

Soybean Snacks: Pull pods from stems. Boil pods in salt water 5 to 10 minutes. They should be soft, but not mushy. Eat as you would eat peanuts for snacks.

Baked Soybeans

Yield: 12 servings

9 c fresh soybeans
1-1/2 t dry mustard

6 T molasses
1 T salt
3 c water
3/4 lb. salt pork or bacon, diced

Mix all ingredients together except salt pork. Place that on top. Bake at 350°F for 2 to 2-1/2 hours.

Freezes well.

Soybean Chili

Yield: 6 to 8 servings

1-1/2 lb. ground beef
1/4 c onion, chopped
3 c tomato purée
1 T chili powder
1-1/2 t salt
1-1/2 c water
4 c fresh soybeans

Brown meat and onion together. Add all ingredients except beans. Simmer slowly for 45 minutes. Add beans and cook until done.

Freezes well.

Squash

Yellow squash can be frozen by this method: Blanch 1/2—inch pieces in boiling water for three minutes; plunge in ice water for three minutes; package in air-right plastic or glass container; seal and freeze. It may be boiled until tender, mashed and frozen.

Zucchini may be prepared for serving; blanched in boiling water for just one minute, plunged in ice water for one minute, packaged and frozen.

Hint: Use mashed yellow squash in any of the pumpkin recipes calling for mashed pumpkin.

Pork Stuffed Zucchini

Yield: 8 servings

8 medium-size zucchini
2 c water
1 t salt
8 pork sausages
1/2 c Cheddar cheese, grated
1 c catsup

Wash zucchini and remove both ends. Parboil whole in salted water for three minutes; drain. Cut a gash lengthwise in each zucchini, then place one sausage in each, tucking the ends into the zucchini.

Place in a baking pan, sprinkle with cheese and pour catsup over. Pour water in baking dish, about 1/4-inch deep. Bake in moderate oven (350°F) for 45 minutes, or until sausage is thoroughly cooked and browned.

Abalone and Zucchini Soup

Yield: 8 servings

1 lb. pork, sliced
2 zucchini, sliced 1/8" thick
1 can abalone
7 c liquid (juice from canned abalone
  plus water to make 7 cups)
2 t salt
dash of pepper
1/4 t MSG
1 T shoyu

Fry pork until brown. Add liquid and cook for 15 to 20 minutes. Add seasonings. Add zucchini and cook 10 to 15 minutes, until squash is soft. Add sliced abalone.

Steamed Squash with Pork Hash Filling

Yield: 6 servings when accompanying other foods

1 Chinese squash (looks like fuzzy watermelon)
1 lb. ground pork
6 water chestnuts, chopped
1/4 c green onions, cut in 1/4" lengths
4 t shoyu
2 t sugar
2 t sherry
1/2 t salt
2 t cornstarch
1/4 t MSG

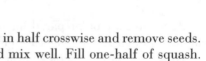

Scrape fuzzy skin off squash with knife. Cut in half crosswise and remove seeds. Combine pork with remaining ingredients and mix well. Fill one-half of squash. Cover with top of squash. Place in steamer and cook 45 minutes. To serve, remove top and cut filled section in pieces.

Hamburger Gravy with Zucchini

Yield: 4 servings

1 lb. hamburger
1/4 c bacon, chopped
1 medium onion, chopped
1 T shoyu
1-1/2 t salt
1/2 t MSG
1/2 t sugar
3 medium-size zucchini, sliced 1/4" thick
2 T flour
1 c water

Sauté bacon slightly, add hamburger and onion. Cook until hamburger is almost done. Add seasonings and zucchini. Simmer until zucchini is tender. Combine flour and water; add to hamburger and cook to thicken.

Pickled Portuguese Squash

Use pipinalish squash, sliced thin in place of daikon in takuwan. Add a little hot pepper for taste, a little more food coloring (yellow) than usual.

Squash Corn Cakes

Yield: 15 cakes, 2-1/2" in diameter

I egg
1/2 t salt
1/4 t pepper
1/4 t MSG
I T onion, finely chopped
I c cream style corn
I c cooked zucchini, well drained and mashed
3 T flour or more

Beat egg, salt, pepper and monosodium glutamate together, then add onion, corn, and zucchini. Stir in flour. Add more flour if necessary to make mixture the consistency of pancake batter. Drop mixture by tablespoonful onto a hot greased griddle. Fry until golden brown on both sides.

Zucchini in Sour Cream

Yield: 4 servings

I lb. zucchini
I 7 oz. can button mushrooms
2/3 c sour cream
1/2 t salt
1/8 t pepper
I T olives, finely chopped

Wash zucchini, remove both ends and slice. Drain juice from mushrooms, then steam sliced zucchini in mushroom juice for 10 minutes, or until just tender; drain. Combine zucchini with mushrooms, sour cream, salt and pepper. Reheat, but do not boil. Turn into serving dish and sprinkle with chives. Serve immediately.

Star Fruit

Matured fruit is about four inches long, has a tender, edible skin. When sliced crosswise, this fruit is a perfect star. Used in fruit salads or dessert. Sieve or blend pulp to make juice. It can be made into a sliced preserve to be used or given at Christmas.

STAR FRUIT JELLY

3 c star fruit juice
1/4 c lemon juice
yellow food coloring
1 pkg. powdered pectin
4-1/2 c sugar

Bring juices, food coloring and pectin to a rolling boil. Add sugar, bring back to boil and boil hard for one minute. Pour into sterilized jelly jars. Cover with thin coating of melted paraffin.

Surinam Cherries

Fruit is bright red when ready to be picked. This small-ridged cherry may be used in salads, jellies, or fruit desserts. The juice combines well with other fruit juices and adds a delightful color. Use for fruit ices or sherbet.

❖ Slice or mash and sprinkle with granulated sugar. Package quickly and freeze. It develops a bitter taste if left to stand very long.

Calories: 1 cup—38

SURINAM CHERRY CHIFFON PIE

1 baked pie crust, cooled
1 T unflavored gelatin
1/4 c cold water
4 eggs, separated
1 c sugar
1/2 c surinam cherry juice
1/2 t salt
whipped cream (optional)

Soften gelatin in water. Beat yolks and add 1/2 cup sugar, juice and salt. Cook until thick, stirring constantly. Add softened gelatin and stir thoroughly. Cool. Beat whites until frothy. Gradually beat in remaining 1/2 cup sugar and beat until mixture holds soft peaks. Fold into cooled egg yolk mixture and fill baked pie shell. Chill. Top with whipped cream. Decorate with surinam cherry halves before serving. For a more flavorful pie, add 1/4 cup surinam cherry pulp when adding gelatin.

Sweet Potatoes and Yams

May be frozen after being cooked and mashed. Use in the recipes calling for cooked, mashed pumpkin.

SWEET POTATO CAKE

1-1/2 c cooking oil
2 c sugar
4 eggs, separated
4 t hot water
2-1/2 c sifted cake flour

3 t baking powder
1/4 t salt
1 t ground cinnamon
1 t round nutmeg
1-1/2 c raw sweet potatoes, grated
1 c nuts, chopped
1 t vanilla

Combine cooking oil and sugar and beat until smooth. Add egg yolks and beat well. Add hot water, then dry ingredients which have been sifted together. Stir in potatoes, nuts and vanilla and beat well. Beat egg whites until stiff and fold into mixture. Bake in three greased 8-inch layer cake pans at 350°F for 25 to 30 minutes. Cool and frost with peach frosting.

Add 1/2 cup water if batter seems too stiff.

Peach Frosting

1 c butter or margarine
2 c powdered sugar
1 c peaches, well drained and mashed

Cream butter and powdered sugar, then add peaches.

Sweet Potato Chips

2-1/4 c sweet potatoes, thinly sliced (3/4lb.)
1 T powdered sugar
1 qt. oil or fat for frying

Pare and slice the potatoes crosswise into very thin slices. Soak in cold water 15 minutes, and drain thoroughly. Fry in deep fat at 350°F until potatoes are a delicate brown. Drain on absorbent paper, sprinkle with powdered sugar or salt. Serve with a salad or as a vegetable.

Sweet Potato Salad

4 or 5 sweet potatoes, cooked and diced
1 c celery, chopped
1/4 c green onion, chopped
1 can mandarin oranges, drained
1/2 c sour cream or yogurt
1/2 c mayonnaise
salt and pepper to taste

Combine vegetables and mandarin oranges. Mix mayonnaise with sour cream or yogurt and seasonings. Serve well chilled. Roasted almonds may be added.

Sweet Potato Tops

Boil young sweet potato tops in small amount of water until tender (about three minutes). Serve topped with chopped tomato, MSG, salt and shoyu.

Yam Stuffed Bananas

Yield: 6 servings

6 large bananas, green tipped
2-1/2 c cooked yams, mashed
I t salt
I T brown sugar
I small can crushed pineapple, drained
1/2 c salted peanuts, chopped
1/3 c cooked bacon, chopped

Wash bananas, split lengthwise on one side; do NOT cut through ends or opposite side of bananas. Remove banana pulp and mash. Keep banana shells. Combine banana pulp, yams, salt, sugar, pineapple, nuts and bacon; blend. Fill banana shells with the mixture. Top with additional peanuts if desired. Bake in a moderate oven (350°F) for 15 minutes.

Yam Nests with Green Beans

Yield: 6 servings

I lb. hot yams, mashed
I egg, beaten
1/2 t salt
dash of pepper
1/2 lb. cooked green beans
2 T butter, melted
1/4 c peanuts, chopped

Combine mashed yams, egg, salt and pepper. Form six nests on ungreased baking sheet. Place spoonful of green beans in each nest. Drizzle each nest with 1 teaspoon butter and sprinkle with chopped nuts. Bake 10 to 15 minutes in 350°F oven. Serve hot.

French Fried Sweet Potatoes

3 medium cold, boiled sweet potatoes
salt or sugar
fat for frying

Be sure the sweet potatoes are cold so that they can be cut without breaking apart. Cut sweet potatoes lengthwise into slices 1/2-inch thick, and then cut slices into long strips 1/2-inch wide. Fry in deep fat heated to 375°F from one to two minutes or until golden brown. Drain on absorbent paper. Sprinkle with salt or sugar, as desired.

Tamarind

Clusters of green seedpods hang from a large tamarind tree. When green, they can be chopped skin and all to make an unusual flavoring for foods. Filipinos use them especially with fish. The outer shells become brown and crusty similar to the lychee upon ripening. It is eaten at this stage by just removing the shell and eating the inner flesh. The taste is sour like the sour preserved seeds. Cook with brown sugar to make sweet-sour seeds.

Tangerine

❖ Tangerine juice freezes very well.

TANGERINE JELLY

2-3/4 c fresh tangerine juice
I box powdered pectin OR I bottle liquid pectin
sugar

Follow directions on box or bottle of pectin for frozen tangerine concentrate. Use fresh juice instead of concentrate and water.

Taro and Taro Leaves (Luau)

Hawaiian Taro (Apu) may be used in any way in which potatoes are used: creamed, scalloped, fried, baked, mashed and boiled. To insure thorough cooking, it is best to boil corms before frying or baking. Boil before peeling to avoid itchy feeling on hands. One pound taro yields four servings.

BOILED TARO

2 to 3 lb. taro
I t salt
boiling water

Scrub taro corms thoroughly. Pour sufficient boiling water over them to half-cover corms. Cover and boil 1-1/2 hours or until tender. If taro is to be used for poi, cook until very tender. Peel cooked taro and use as desired.

TARO CAKES

Yield: 4 to 5 servings

I large taro corm (approx. I-1/4 lb. will yield
** 2 c boiled and mashed)**
I T milk
I T butter or margarine
I egg yolk
I t salt
1/8 t pepper
2–3 T flour
I–2 T fat

Boil the taro corm in the skin until tender, following directions above. Peel and mash while hot, since it is difficult to mash cold taro. Add all ingredients except flour and fat and mix well. Shape into flat cakes, roll in flour and sauté, using 1 tablespoon fat at the beginning and adding more as needed.

Variation: For variety in texture as well as flavor, one or all of the following ingredients may be added to the above recipe:

1 T green onion, chopped
1 T celery, finely chopped
1 T parsley, chopped
1 strip bacon, cooked until crisp and chopped

Poi

Put poi in large bowl. Mix with hand, adding a little water at a time. Continue mixing and adding water until of desired consistency. To store in refrigerator, add think layer of water over the poi to prevent drying.

❖To freeze, put in containers and freeze. When ready to use, place in open foil package and steam. Mix more water into poi for proper consistency.

Calories: 1 cup—161

Chinese Taro may also be used in dishes calling for potato or other types of taro.

TARO CHIPS

Peel raw taro corms and slice thin with slicer. Deep fry in oil heated to 380°F. Drain on paper towels and salt generously. These may be frozen in jars for later use.

TARO BISCUITS

Yield: 16 small biscuits

1 c cooked taro, mashed
1/4 c fat
1-1/2 c flour
3 t baking powder
2 t sugar
1/2 t salt
1 egg
1/4 c milk

Combine the cold taro and fat in a mixing bowl. When thoroughly blended add the dry ingredients which have been sifted together. Blend the ingredients with a pastry blender or two knives. Add the beaten egg and milk and mix thoroughly. Place the dough on a lightly floured board and pat it with the fingers to a thickness of 1/2 inch. Cut the dough with a lightly floured biscuit cutter, place biscuits on a lightly floured pan and bake for 15 to 20 minutes in a hot oven (425°F).

TARO ROLLS

2 yeast cakes
1/2 c warm water
2/3 c shortening
3/4 c sugar
1-1/4 T salt
1 c warm milk
3 eggs, beaten

I c taro, mashed
8 c flour
sesame seeds
I egg, beaten, to be used to brush the top of the rolls

Cream sugar and shortening. Add eggs, mashed taro, salt, milk and yeast cakes which have been soaked in 1/2 cup warm water. Then add the flour to make stiff dough. Place on lightly floured board and knead until smooth. Place in a well-greased bowl and let rise until double its size. Make into rolls and brush the tops of the rolls with beaten egg and sprinkle with sesame seeds. Let rise again until double their size. Bake 15 minutes in preheated 375°F oven.

Japanese Taro (Dasheen or Araimo) is used in many tasty Japanese dishes such as Nishime and Miso Soup, or is fried with pork and shoyu.

BUTTERED ARAIMO

Select small Japanese taro. Wash and place in saucepan with 1/2 to 1 cup water and cook 40 to 50 minutes, or until tender. Drain; cut a small piece from one end and gently squeeze the opposite end, and the taro will slip out of its skin. Season with salt and pepper and serve with butter or margarine.

Taro Leaves (Luau) and **Stems** can be used as any green vegetable but must be cooked longer to release the calcium oxalate crystals which cause an itchy feeling in mouth and throat. Some fat added during cooking will speed the destruction of crystals. Add bacon fat, coconut milk or butter and serve as you would spinach. Make Cream of Luau Soup or Spinach Soufflé using leaves that have been cooked 45 minutes in salted water.

CHICKEN LUAU

Yield: 10 servings

1–2-1/2 lb. stewing chicken, cut in 1-1/2-inch pieces
2 T butter
4 c water
I t salt
50 luau leaves
I T salt
2 c water
3 c coconut milk

Sauté chicken in butter. Add 4 cups water and simmer until tender (2-1/2 hours). Season with salt. Remove stems from luau leaves; wash thoroughly. Strip skin from stem with knife. Cook leaves with 2 cups water and salt over medium heat for one hour; drain. Combine chicken, luau leaves and coconut milk. Heat thoroughly and serve.

BAKED FISH WITH TARO LEAVES

I whole fish (2 lb. opakapaka preferred) OR I pkg. frozen cod, thawed
4 ti leaves

4 luau leaves
I caraimo, parboiled (10 min.), peeled and sliced
I large or 2 small tomatoes, sliced
I stalk celery, cut in I" pieces
I sprig green onion, cut in I" pieces
salt to taste (I–2 t)

Lay two ti leaves on a piece of foil large enough to overlap baking dish. Place two taro leaves on ti leaves. Arrange fillets or whole fish on leaves and add vegetables around fish. Sprinkle salt over all. Cover with remaining taro leaves and then ti leaves. Place another piece of foil over all and seal by overlapping bottom foil over edge of top one. Bake for one hour at 375°F.

Laulau

Yield: 20 laulaus

7 lb. brisket, cut in 2" pieces
3 lb. pork butt or belly, cut in 2" pieces
3/4 c Hawaiian salt
2 T liquid smoke
60-70 luau leaves, stems stripped, or spinach
40 ti leaves or foil
string
10 sweet potatoes, scrubbed

Add 1/2 cup salt and 1 tablespoon smoke to beef, mix thoroughly. Mix pork with remaining 1/4 cup salt and 1 tablespoon smoke. Remove stems from luau leaves; wash leaves thoroughly. Strip skin from stems with knife. Arrange three luau leaves, the largest on the bottom, on the palm of the hand. Place pork and beef cubes in center of leaves. Top with four or five stems and two more leaves. Prepare each ti leaf by cutting partially through the stiff back rib, about one-half way up. Strip down to stem. Place laulau on the end of a ti leaf and wrap tightly. Wrap another ti leaf around in opposite direction forming a flat package. Tie with string or fibrous part of ti leaves. Steam four to six hours. Add sweet potatoes for last hour.

Note: To steam in electric roaster, add 3 quarts water. Set temperature control at 350°F, place rack above water and put laulaus on rack when steaming point is reached. When steaming thoroughly, lower temperature to 300°F. Replenish water at end of 2-1/2 hours.

Ti Leaves

Green ti leaves are used for many purposes, including "grass" skirts, haku-type leis, tray liners, dishes, and in cooking. They impart a wonderful flavor to meats and fish that are wrapped for cooking. If ti leaves are not available, grape leaves, banana leaves, spinach, corn husks or foil may be substituted.

To wrap laulau, fish or other foods, first remove the rib of the leaf. Starting from tip, roll leaf forward until rib prevents this. With knife, cut through rib only. Roll leaf carefully away from rib.

Cut squares of ti leaves and use as serves for Haupia, cake or cookies.

Fish in Ti Leaves

Yield: 6 servings

6 whole fish or fillets
Hawaiian salt to taste
12 ti leaves

Sprinkle each serving of fish with salt. Wrap each in two ti leaves. Place on broiler rack and broil until fish is cooked.

Kalua Pig in Pot

Yield: 6 servings

3 lb. Boston butt
1 T Hawaiian salt
1 T liquid smoke
6 ti leaves
foil
6 sweet potatoes

Rub pork with salt. Brush with smoke. Wrap in ti leaves first, then foil. Place on rack in large, deep pot. Add one inch of water. Simmer for three hours. Replenish water when necessary. Open foil, place sweet potatoes around pork. Seal again. Steam one hour longer. Shred pork, toss with 1 teaspoon Hawaiian salt. Pour juice from foil package over the pork. Garnish with sliced sweet potatoes.

Hint: If pork is dry, add water and salt. Heat thoroughly.

Tofu

Tofu is soybean curd sole in white blocks. It adds a good supply of calcium to the diet. Mash and add to tuna dishes; chop fine and add to omelets; add to tempura dough for fish patties, or pupus; slice thin and fry until golden brown and serve with meat and vegetables.

❖ Tofu becomes spongy after freezing, but may be used in a cooked shoyu dish.

Calories: One-fourth block—72

Pork Tofu

1 lb. pork
1 T oil
1/2 c shoyu
1/4 c water
1/3 c sugar
1 medium onion, sliced
1 small piece ginger, crushed
1 tofu, cubed
1/4 t MSG
12 green onions, cut in 2" lengths

Thinly slice pork into 1-to 2-inch pieces; brown in hot fat. Add shoyu, water, sugar, onion and ginger. Bring to a boil and simmer for five minutes. Add tofu and MSG; simmer gently for a few minutes. Just before serving add green onions.

Tomato

❖ Tomato juice freezes well. Boil halved tomatoes three to four minutes, mashing to release juice. Strain and fill jars to one-half inch from top. Cover tightly and freeze. Quartered ripe tomatoes can be frozen for stewing later.

BONNIE'S TOMATO SOUP FRENCH DRESSING

1 can tomato soup
1/2 c sugar
3/4 c vinegar
1 t salt
1/2 t paprika
1/2 t pepper
2 t prepared mustard
1 T Worcestershire sauce

Mix ingredients in a bowl and slowly add 1-1/2 cups oil. Place in glass container with six cloves of garlic. This will keep in the refrigerator.

GREEN TOMATO CHUTNEY

Yield: 4 pints

8 lb. green tomatoes
3/4 c onions, chopped
1 c brown sugar
1 T peppercorns or 1/4 t pepper
1/4 c salt
1/4 c mixed pickling spices
1/2 clove garlic
3 c white vinegar
1 lb. apples
3/4 c white raisins
3/4 c sugar

Core and quarter tomatoes. Combine in large kettle with onions, brown sugar, salt, peppercorns, pickling spices, garlic and vinegar. Boil mixture for 15 minutes. Put through colander or food mill (this strains out whole spices). Return to heat; simmer four hours, until thick and clear.

Core and chop apples. Combine with raisins and sugar. Simmer until fruit is soft. Stir into tomato mixture, and pour into hot, sterilized pint jars.

GREEN TOMATO PICKLES

Leave stems on. Pack in sterilized quart jars. To each quart add 1 clove garlic, 1 stalk celery, 1 hot green pepper and 1 head dill. Combine 2 quarts water, 1 quart vinegar, 1 cup salt. Cook five minutes. Fill jars to one-half inch from top. Seal.

LOMI SALMON

Yield: 6 servings

1/2 lb. salt salmon
2 large ripe tomatoes, diced
1 small round onion, chopped
1 sprig green onion, chopped
2 cubes ice

Select salmon with thick meat. Soak in cold water overnight and drain. Take off skin and free from bones. Pick into small pieces and put in bowl. Add tomatoes, onion and ice and lomi with hands until all are in small pieces. Chill until watery.

Tree Tomato

This is a seasonal elongated dark red fruit. It looks like a Christmas ornament. It is native to New Zealand but grows in Kula. High vitamin C content, delightful taste and color make it a valuable and versatile fruit.

Peel by immersing in boiling water for a few minutes before peeling. It is easier to halve it and scoop out the pulp. Use as a substitute for tomatoes in casseroles, in place of guava pulp in the guava recipes (try chiffon pie), in chutney and in fruit desserts.

Because of the texture, tree tomatoes do not freeze well in slices. You may mash it and freeze for use in pies, jam, jelly, sauce, etc. The juice, either cooked for jelly or raw, freezes very well.

TREE TOMATO JUICE

Scoop pulp from skin of ripe tree tomato into blender. Add 1/2 cup water to blender container. Blend until smooth. Combine with pineapple, orange or lemon juice for a pretty pink drink.

TREE TOMATO JELLY

6 lb. tree tomatoes, almost ripe
6 c water
10–12 c sugar
1 lemon, squeezed

Skin or scoop pulp from fruit. Slice into large pot. Boil with water until a soft pulp forms. Strain through jelly bag overnight. Do not squeeze bag or jelly will be cloudy. Bring juice to a boil, add one cup sugar for each cup juice. Boil briskly for one-half hour, then add juice of the lemon. Skim off foam. Pour into hot, sterilized jars and cover with 1/8-inch melted paraffin.

MOLDED TREE TOMATO SALAD

6 small tree tomatoes (3 large)
1/2 c water
1 pkg. lemon gelatin

Peel tree tomatoes, cut in slices. Cook on low heat with water until soft. Add lemon gelatin. Stir until dissolved and fruit is mashed. Pour into mold. Chill and serve on lettuce greens.

TREE TOMATO JAM

4 lb. fruit (8 c)
4 lb. sugar (8 c)
4 T lemon juice

Peel fruit, cut into small pieces. Sprinkle with half the sugar. Let stand overnight. Next morning, boil for 20 minutes, then add remaining sugar and lemon juice. Boil until ready to set. Skim off foam. Pour into hot, sterilized jars and seal with 1/8-inch melted paraffin.

TREE TOMATO AND APPLE PIE

pastry for crust, 9" pie
3 c cooking apples, sliced
2 c tree tomatoes, peeled and sliced
1 c sugar
1 t cinnamon
1/8 t salt
2 T butter or margarine

Combine apples, tree tomatoes, sugar, cinnamon and salt. Pour into pastry-lined pan. Dot with butter. Cover with top crust and flute edges. Glaze top with water or milk and sprinkle with sugar. Bake at 425°F for 15 minutes and 350°F for 35 minutes.

Bacon and Tree Tomatoes

Try a sandwich of these two. Fry bacon and thin slices of tree tomatoes together.

Water Chestnuts

Use in steamed pork hash, chop suey or other vegetable dishes.
❖ Freezes well.

TEMPURA DOUGH PUPUS

2 lb. tempura dough (raw fish cake)
1 lb. ground pork
1 T shoyu
dash of MSG
1 6 oz. can water chestnuts
1/4 c green onions, chopped
2 T sugar
1/2 t five spice

Fry pork until done, seasoning with shoyu and MSG during frying. Mix with remaining ingredients, form into balls and deep fry. This basic recipe can be varied by adding ham or rolling in egg and crumbs.

Water Chestnuts in Bacon

1 6 oz. can water chestnuts
1 T salt
1 T Worcestershire sauce
2 T lemon juice
1 lb. bacon

Slice chestnuts in half crosswise. Soak in mixture of salt, Worcestershire sauce and lemon juice for at least one hour. Wrap one-third slice bacon around chestnut half and secure with toothpick. Broil until bacon is crisp. Serve hot.

Watercress
. . . .

❖ Does **not** freeze well. Add watercress to either vegetable or fruit salads. Mold it in Perfection Salad.

Flank Steak with Watercress

Yield: 6 servings

1 flank steak
1/2 t salt
dash of pepper
1-1/2 c watercress, chopped
3/4 c nuts, chopped
2 T shortening
2 medium onions, sliced
2 medium carrots, sliced
1/4 c water or meat stock

Lightly score the steak on both sides; season with salt and pepper. Combine the watercress and nuts; spread on the steak. Roll in jelly roll fashion and fasten with string or skewer. Brown on all sides in melted shortening. Turn to low heat and cook about 1-1/2 hours or until the meat is tender. During the last half hour of cooking, add the carrots and onions and the liquid.

Watercress Shitashi

1 bunch watercress
1 T toasted sesame seeds
2 T sugar
1/2 t MSG
2 T shoyu
1 T mirin

Pour boiling water over watercress to wilt. Press out excess water. Cut in 1-1/2-inch pieces. Arrange on plate. Pour sauce of mashed sesame seeds, sugar, MSG, shoyu and mirin over watercress. Serve as salad at room temperature.

WATERCRESS TEMPURA

Yield: 5 servings

I egg
1/2 c cornstarch
1/2 c flour
I t salt
1/2 t MSG
I bunch watercress

Beat egg thoroughly with a fork. Do not use an egg beater. Pour egg into a measuring cup and add enough water to make 3/4 cup. Combine dry ingredients and mix well. Pour egg mixture into dry ingredients and mix well by folding. Do not beat, the little lumps do not matter.

For best results, chill the batter in the refrigerator for at least one hour before using. Wash watercress, drain dry, and cut into one-inch pieces. Put watercress into batter and mix well. Drop this mixture by tablespoonful and fry in very hot deep fat until golden brown and crunchy.

CREAM OF WATERCRESS SOUP

3 c milk
2 c watercress, finely chopped
I small onion, chopped
I c cooked potato, finely diced
I t Worcestershire sauce
I t salt
dash of pepper

Combine milk, watercress, onion and potato in saucepan. Simmer on low heat for 25 minutes. Add seasonings and serve with croutons.

CHINESE STYLE WATERCRESS

I bunch watercress, cleaned and drained
I T oil
I pinch Hawaiian salt
I clove garlic, crushed

Cut watercress in three to four-inch lengths. Heat fry pan very hot. Add oil, then garlic and Hawaiian salt. Add watercress and stir-fry just until slightly wilted. Should still be crisp.

ANN'S SUKIYAKI (HEKKA)

3 lb. Island chicken, beef or pork
4 T butter
I 6-1/3 oz. can boiled Japanese mushrooms
    (matsutake) drained, but liquid reserved
I 8-1/2 oz. can bamboo shoots (takenoko)
I pkg. pepeiao (fungus)
I pkg. konyaku OR I 8-1/2 oz. can
    shirataki (alimentary paste)

1 round onion
12 sprigs green onion
1 bunch watercress

Shoyu mixture:
3/4 c raw sugar
1 c shoyu
1/4 c mirin or beer
1/2 t MSG

Either chop or debone and slice chicken in bite-size pieces. Use strips of beef or pork. Stir-fry half of chicken or meat in 2 tablespoons butter about five minutes. Add half shoyu mixture. Cook 5 to 10 minutes. Add mushrooms, bamboo shoots, pepeiao, konyaku. Cook five minutes; add mushroom liquid or beef if too dry. Add round and green onions and watercress. Stir-cook briefly and serve hot.

Sukiyaki should be cooked at the table. Guests sit around and eat as food is cooked. Usually a hibachi is used, but the electric fry pan works well. Sukiyaki may be eaten dipped in raw egg in individual bowls. Tofu may also be added.

Wi
. . . .

Pronounced **vee**, this fruit is also known as Otaheite apple. It is the size of a common guava and is yellow in color when ripe. The large, rough seed is the distinguishing characteristic of this fruit. All the normal treatments can be given this fruit, but it is best just eaten in season out of hand.

Wine
. . . .

Maui is known for Tedeschi's Pineapple Wine. The drinks below are just a beginning of ways to use **Maui Blanc**. Use it in all recipes in this book in place of grape wine, sherry or bourbon, especially Beef Broccoli, Haole Hekka, Teriyaki Sauce and Beef with Long Rice. Add it to other meat dishes to enhance flavor, especially Pork Tofu, Hamburger and Long Rice, Jelly Fish, Hamburger Gravy with Zucchini and Tempura Dough Pupus. Our thanks to Emil Tedeschi for these beverage recipes.

*For stronger drinks, use less ice.

FROZEN PINEAPPLE WINE JOHN-JOHN

Yield: 4 servings.

ice
1 c pineapple juice
1/2 c pineapple wine
1/4 c coconut syrup

Fill blender one-half full* of ice, pour in juice, wine and syrup. Blend.

FROZEN PINEAPPLE DAIQUIRI

Yield: 4 servings

ice
1 c pineapple juice
juice of 1/2 lemon
1/2 t sugar
1/2 c pineapple wine

Fill blender one-half full* of ice, pour in pineapple juice, lemon juice, sugar and pineapple wine. Blend.

FROZEN STRAWBERRY DAIQUIRI

Yield: 4 servings

ice
1 c strawberry daiquiri mix
1/2 c pineapple wine

Fill blend one-half full* of ice, pour in daiquiri mix and wine. Blend.

Ethnic Foods Index

Index
. . . . . .

Haupia with Fruit, 29
Hawaiian Fruit Cake, 55
Hawaiian Harvest Cake, 42
Homemade Biscuit Mix, 24

J

Jams, Jellies, etc.
    Green Tomato Chutney, 98
    Guava Jelly, 44
    Kumquat Marmalade, 46
    Loquat Jelly, 51
    Mango Butter, 58
    Mango Jam, 57
    Mango Chutney, 60
    Mango Marmalade, 58
    Mrs. Young's Loquat Jam, 50
    Pineapple Chutney, 73
    Pineapple Jam, 73
    Plum Jelly, 74
    Poha Jam, 76
    Preserved Kumquats, 46
    Rhubarb Jam, 81
    Roselle Jelly, 85
    Shredded Mango, 59
    Star Fruit Jelly, 89
    Tangerine Jelly, 93
    Tree Tomato Jam, 100
    Tree Tomato Jelly, 99
    Uncooked Berry Jam, 18
Jello Kanten, 14
Jiffy Fish, 39

K

Kalua Pig in Pot, 97
Kalua Pig with Chinese Vegetables, 11
Kamaboko Sushi, 82
Kimch'i, 22
Kimpira Gobo, 39
Kumquat Marmalade, 46

L

Laulau, 96
Lauya—See Chicken with Papaya, 64
Lemon Meringue Pie for the
   Freezer, 47
Lemon Milkshake, 48
Lilikoi Muffins, 66

Limu-Onion Relish, 49
Lomi Salmon, 99
Loquat Jelly, 51
Loquat Pie, 49
Lychee Salad, 53
Lychees with Ham, 53

M

Macadamia Bavarian Cream Pie, 55
Macadamia Cream Pie, 54
Macadamia Sundae Sauce, 55
Main Dishes—See Entrées
Mango Bread, 58
Mango Butter, 58
Mango Chiffon Pie, 59
Mango Chutney, 60
Mango Jam, 57
Mango Marmalade, 58
Mango Seeds, 59
Mango Sherbet, 60
Mary Oh's Pie Crust, 56
Mock Whipped Cream Icing, 14
Molded Sushi, 82
Molded Tree Tomato Salad, 99
Mousakka (Greek), 36
Muffins
    Lilikoi Muffins, 66
    Pumpkin Muffins, 80
    Speedy Carrot Muffins, 23
    Susan's Pineapple Muffins, 73
Mustard Pickles, 34

N

Namasu, 32, 49
Nippy Carrot Nibblers, 24
Nishime (Japanese), 40
No-Roll Coconut Crust, 29

O

Omelets
    Eggplant Omelet, 36
Opihi Limu, 48

P

Papaya and Salted Nut Salad, 64
Papaya Chiffon Pie, 64